Far from the Cliff

Far from the Cliff

——— A Memoir ———

Ray Moisa

RESOURCE *Publications* • Eugene, Oregon

FAR FROM THE CLIFF
A Memoir

Copyright © 2022 Ray Moisa. All rights reserved. Except for brief quotations in critical publications or reviews, no part of this book may be reproduced in any manner without prior written permission from the publisher. Write: Permissions, Wipf and Stock Publishers, 199 W. 8th Ave., Suite 3, Eugene, OR 97401.

Resource Publications
An Imprint of Wipf and Stock Publishers
199 W. 8th Ave., Suite 3
Eugene, OR 97401

www.wipfandstock.com

PAPERBACK ISBN: 978-1-6667-5547-3
HARDCOVER ISBN: 978-1-6667-5548-0
EBOOK ISBN: 978-1-6667-5549-7

11/03/22

Scripture quotations are from the Common Bible: New Revised Standard Version Bible, copyright © 1989 National Council of the Churches of Christ in the United States of America. Used by permission. All rights reserved worldwide.

Dedicated to Elizabeth, Mary, and Suleika,
for inspiring me,
and to Mom, for showing me to the door
and the road to my freedom

Contents

Acknowledgements | ix
The Plague as Transformative Force | 1
   In Beauty I Walk | 3
The Ball of Green Yarn | 4
In the Year of the Plague | 11
Long-Term Care Insurance | 17
What Is Lost and What Is Gained | 18
   Italian Dawn | 20
The Parting of the Red Sea | 22
   dancing with a stranger | 33
Lockdown | 34
Dad | 41
Sonny and Me | 48
Ernie | 60
   until | 64
I'm Santa Claus | 66
Jo Ann | 76
Requiem for a Stranger | 78
Adolescence | 79
Vietnam and the Draft | 83
Stupid Stuff | 85
The Near-Fatal Collision | 90
My Professional Career | 95
The Insidious Scar Tissue of Racism | 100
San Francisco and Bill | 103
The Life of the Nomad | 111

CONTENTS

Another Close Call | 121
Anthony Bourdain and the Art of Travel | 124
Near-Disaster in the High Sierra | 132
My Mother's Unshakeable Faith | 137
The Day I Spent with Muhammad Ali | 149
Long COVID | 151
My Beautiful Big Blue House | 155
   In the House Made of Dawn | 160

Epilogue | 161
Bibliography | 165

Acknowledgements

I WISH TO THANK MY publisher, Wipf and Stock, and their imprint, Resource Publications, for seeing something in my words worth sharing with the world that exists beyond the quiet chambers of my soul.

    I wish to express also my deepest appreciation to my copyeditor, Rebecca Abbott, for the grace and elegance she brought to my clumsy expressions of love and pain, and how she tempered my tears of joy and sorrow with dignity, power, and delight.

The Plague as Transformative Force

On January 31, 2020, the World Health Organization declared the novel coronavirus outbreak a Public Health Emergency of International Concern. After a number of scattered but related cases began to appear across the world from its known origins in Wuhan, China, medical scientists and public health experts in every part of the globe were sounding the alarm and mobilizing efforts to deal with this new virus, which came to be known in the public consciousness as COVID-19.

Exactly one year later, to the very day, I was infected with COVID, and it came down on me hard. It was, in fact, a severe, life-threatening case that laid me at death's door for five weeks, with five days in the ICU, and ultimately transformed my life on many levels. I survived COVID, and I am a better man for it.

But this deadly disease, which I prefer to call "the plague," has killed many millions of people around the world. No country has escaped its deadly grasp. No one is safe. It is, in every sense of the word, a plague, the word that defines an epidemic disease causing a high rate of mortality; also, a disastrous evil or calamity. As of this writing, there is no end in sight for COVID and the world. For me, the plague is an ever-present force in my consciousness. I recall with absolute clarity how I felt in the hospital fighting for my life. And every day and night since then, I thank God I am alive, and I remind myself that I must make the very most out of each and every hour I live.

After I was discharged from the hospital, my doctor told me I should have been dead after twelve days with all the damage the plague had done to me. Ever since then, I have sought to resolve for myself the mystery of why I was allowed to beat such catastrophic odds. I have focused myself on finding new purpose in my life, at a time when I believed I had accomplished all my life goals and fully met my purpose in this world. The plague taught me that I was mistaken on that point.

Everything for me has changed for the better since I beat the plague, and I vow to remember always the lessons of this awful and yet bountiful experience. I was pulled back—far from the cliff—on the day my doctor told me I was well enough to return home after my near-death ordeal. I am a survivor. I am born again. This is my story. This is my life—the old one and the new one.

> *And I believe in the forgiveness of sins, the resurrection of the body, and the life everlasting.*
> —*The Apostles' Creed*

In Beauty I Walk

In beauty I walk
With beauty before me I walk
With beauty behind me I walk
With beauty above me I walk
With beauty around me I walk
It has become beauty again

Today I will walk out
Everything negative will leave me
I will be as I was before
I will have a cool breeze over my body

I will have a light body
I will be happy forever
Nothing will hinder me

I walk with beauty before me
I walk with beauty behind me
I walk with beauty below me
I walk with beauty around me
My words will be beautiful

In beauty all day long may I walk
Through the returning seasons may I walk
With beauty before me may I walk
With beauty below me may I walk
With beauty above me may I walk
With beauty all around me may I walk

In old age wandering on a trail of beauty, lively, may I walk
In old age wandering on a trail of beauty, living again, may I walk
My words will be beautiful

—*Traditional Dineh Blessingway Chant*

The Ball of Green Yarn

There are lots of stories and fairy tales that grown-ups told us when we were children. Santa Claus. The Easter bunny. The tooth fairy. Cucuy (the bogeyman in Mexican American and Latin American cultures). But there is one "mythical" being, our guardian angel, that we learned about when we were kids who became for me more real in my life—not less—as time went on.

All the other impossible fables of childhood disappeared from reality one by one as I got older, as well they should.

I mean, really, a giant bunny that hops around hiding multicolored eggs around the house or outside in the grass and bushes? Or a big fat man with a long white beard all dressed in red who leaves toys for us under the Christmas tree and who goes riding all over the world in a sleigh visiting every home in the whole world all in one night? And Cucuy and the tooth fairy and all the rest, evaporating in the light of day, banished like the stars before the morning sun.

Indeed, these fabrications the adult world foisted upon our impressionable and gullible little psyches could never really be expected to stand up to the scrutiny of even the youngest inquiring minds. I firmly believed in the existance of Santa Claus, but even before I entered first grade, I remember being confused and puzzled by the simple fact that all the things I wanted for Christmas were sitting on store shelves.

Did Santa's elves make the gifts and then ship them to the Sears Roebuck near me? Or how could Santa deliver our toys if we didn't have a chimney? Or what about that time I noticed that a box of PAAS food dye had suddenly appeared in our kitchen cupboard just days before Easter, and why were there a dozen eggs sitting in the fridge this week if we never ate eggs for breakfast?

Things just did not add up to the stories we were told, I recall thinking when I was six years old. It was all very confusing to an innocent yet probing little mind. And, over time, as we compared our information and suspicions with the other kids in the neighborhood, these fictions soon collapsed under the weight of their own absurdity.

But my guardian angel was another matter altogether. In my mother's bedroom in the projects where we grew up, there was a small print, maybe five by eight inches, of a little boy and girl (I used to imagine it was my little sister and I) playing on a grassy knoll dangerously close to the edge of a steep cliff. Behind them stood a guardian angel, big as a grown-up, with a full-length white robe and pure white wings that nearly touched the ground. The angel's wings were spread out, enveloping the children and keeping them far from the edge of the cliff. The caption in the picture read: *"I will watch over you always."*

That religious icon a lifetime ago from the projects in the barrio far away has stayed with me all these years. Today, that image remains vivid still, in my head and in my heart. There are so many things I recall in my life, so many memories I cannot shake, will never forget. That simple picture remains for me so much more than a static image from my past, a childhood memory.

I believed then that I had a guardian angel always watching over me. I saw myself as the little boy in the picture, surrounded by the protective wings of a supernatural being, someone who would never leave my side, someone I could trust forever. *I will watch over you always*—words I took to heart, words I always believed, words that never seemed to fail me, even in my darkest hours—especially in my darkest hours.

I can tell you the very first time those words were affirmed to me; the very moment when I realized that the guardian angel pictured on my mother's bedroom wall was someone real, not merely an article of faith or religious dogma or childhood fairy tale, not another lie the grown-ups told us.

Those words became real and true for me, I am sure, because the moment that angel came off the wall and became actual fact occurred when I was still very young and impressionable and willing to fully accept that what I had witnessed with my own eyes and touched with my own hands was genuine, solid, and there for me, now and always. I was too young at that time to be cynical. And now, I have seen too much to be cynical.

I was in the second grade, walking to school one morning in East Los Angeles. We lived in the Estrada Courts housing project. I guess today it would be called the hood, but back then, we called it the projects. We—that is, Mom, my kid sister Jo Ann, and my older brother, Sonny (no one called him by his real name, Eddie)—lived just a few blocks from our grammar school, Resurrection School, and a few blocks further up Lorena Street was our church, Resurrection Church.

Like every other Mexican American family in our parish in the 1950s, we were devout Roman Catholics. Our entire lives revolved around the church, not just on Sundays but every day at school and in every circle in which we moved. The Roman Catholic Church was our life.

As I walked to class in my school uniform that warm spring morning, I suddenly realized that I had forgotten to bring a ball of yarn that Sister Mary Edna had been telling us all week to take to class by Friday morning for our art projects that week.

On Monday, Sister Mary Edna had distributed to each of us a sheet of mimeographed paper outlined with a simple design—a house, a flower, a tree, a mountain. She reminded us every day to bring a ball of yarn, any color yarn, and on Friday we were going to sew yarn into our paper, taking the appropriate colors from the big basket filling up with balls of yarn the students had been bringing in all week. As each child brought in their contribution of yarn day by day throughout the week, Sister Mary Edna marked her gradebook to show which students had completed this key step of the project.

Every day that week I had forgotten to ask my mom for some yarn. "Forgotten" is actually a misnomer. I am pretty sure I was not remembering because I knew we did not have yarn in the house, and I understood at some fundamental level that to ask Mom to buy me yarn for this assignment was out of the question, since we barely had enough money to eat. Living in the projects, without a father around, our only income was what we called state aid (at the time, I used to think the term was *state eight*), the twice-monthly government welfare check.

In recent years, the term *Mother's Day* in the projects has come to mean the first and fifteenth of every month, when the welfare checks arrive in the mail. I remember Mom and us kids anxiously waiting for the mailman to arrive on those two days every month. Memories that last a lifetime. Trauma that haunts me still.

I remember, in particular, those days when we were desperately waiting for Mother's Day and our welfare check to arrive in the mail. Our daily dinner in those difficult times was always the same: boiled pinto beans, rice, and homemade flour tortillas. Standard Mexican food, healthy and wholesome, yes, and very economical.

THE BALL OF GREEN YARN

On those days just before the welfare check arrived, when the money ran out and hunger growled loud and long in our little bellies, my mom would play a game with us at dinner. She would tell us to separate each bean and every little grain of rice on our plates, and to eat them one by one, chewing slowly, bite by bite, so as to make them last longer. She said it would help us get full faster.

Another game she taught us with our food was to imagine it was something else, to fantasize that it was something exotic we never ate, a T-bone steak or a roast chicken, with mashed potatoes and gravy. We would throw ourselves into the fantasy, exclaiming as were slowly chewing our beans and rice, "Oh boy, this steak is so tender"; "This is the best roast chicken I ever ate"; "Can I have some more gravy, please?"

When I was older, in my teen years, I was ashamed of the food we ate. As I began to realize on television that people in the family sitcoms ate steak or roast chicken or a big steaming roast beef on Sundays, I came to feel that the food we ate was "poor people's food." This is what I called it then.

I am ashamed now of those thoughts and feelings, first, because I realize my mom was doing the best she could, but, more importantly, because the food we ate every day—plain oatmeal for breakfast or cream of wheat, a peanut butter sandwich and an apple for lunch, beans and rice and tortillas for dinner—was a very healthy and nutritious diet, critical to the proper development of our young bodies.

We never had sweets except at Halloween or Easter. At Christmas, our stockings lying under the tree would be filled with a big Washington State apple, a navel orange, a banana, and nuts of all kinds. All really nutritious food. Never any chocolate. Never any sweets.

I bless my mom for doing well by us under difficult circumstances. I thank her for teaching me the basics of good nutrition and giving us the healthiest (physical) start possible in our lives. I have never forgotten these lessons she taught me. Today, I still eat oatmeal at breakfast, and rarely eat candy. I eat only nutritious foods. My health is good. I owe my life today to my good health. Literally.

Every now and then, the mother in the "colored family" living down at the end of our block of apartments would make an extra pork chop or two "by mistake," and she would bring it over so we could have a little protein in our diet. Mom divided up the pork chops evenly among us kids, and we devoured them like ravenous puppies.

I mean no disrespect with the term *colored people*. It is how we referred to African Americans in the 1950s. We were not racist, and we certainly did not look down on them. Our projects were populated by Black and Brown folk, and poverty made everyone equal.

In fact, one day I picked up the N-word somewhere outside in the yard, but I had no idea what it meant. When I came home and asked my mother what the word meant, she slapped me halfway across the room, then dragged me crying over to the kitchen sink where she made me drink water with laundry detergent in it, "to clean my mouth out." She yelled at me: "I don't ever want you to use that word again. It's a horrible word."

My mom had lived with a girlfriend in the Deep South for a time during World War II, and she was appalled and disgusted by the racism she had witnessed firsthand there. My mother had a real appreciation for Black folks. They were her idols in music, and she had gone to see Ella Fitzgerald, Billie Holiday, the Platters, and other musical artists perform live. Mom understood how racism was a sickness and an evil in America. She had not a racist bone in her body, and she imparted good values to us in this regard.

I bless that kind and generous African American mom who brought us the "extra" pork chop once in a while. Now you tell me: what mother living in the projects makes "too much food" for her family "by mistake"? I know that woman knew just what she was doing. She made a little extra for us out of a sense of compassion and sharing with us what little food she could afford for her own family. She was an embodiment of my guardian angel.

I think of her today when I give a homeless person on the street some cash or make a donation to the food bank at Christmas. I see that woman's face in every poor person whom I try to help out.

So on that day when the ball of yarn was due, the thought struck me like a punch in the gut: I was coming to school without my yarn and I would get an F for the assignment. Then, quite literally in the next moment, as I was staring down at the sidewalk while I walked and fretting my imminent fate, there it was, at the base of a withered little half-dead tree desperately trying to grow. *A big ball of green yarn.* The greenest, biggest, nicest new ball of yarn ever.

I reached down and snatched up that ball of green yarn and quickly stuck it in my lunch bag, furtively glancing around to see if anyone had seen me, if someone would yell at me to drop the yarn, as if I had stolen it from the display case at the local Woolworth's department store. I knew the yarn was not mine, so it must belong to someone else. I sensed that what I had done was wrong in some way. Catholic guilt was a powerful force to reckon with at the age of seven.

I walked to school carrying my heavy burden of yarn. Initially, it had seemed to be my momentary redemption, a way to avoid a bad grade that day, but then another guilt-driven fear soon consumed my conscience. I was convinced that the yarn belonged to a fellow classmate, some other kid had dropped it on their way to school that morning, and I knew that as soon as I walked up to Sister Mary Edna and produced "my" ball of green yarn, that other student would jump up from his or her desk and yell out, "Hey, that's my yarn!"

It was my own personal version of Emile Zola's *J'accuse*, and there I would stand, exposed and shamed, a thief, a fraud, a big ugly F next to my name in the gradebook. That ball of green yarn got heavier in my sack with every step I took toward school that morning. I almost cursed my apparent good fortune. I didn't know what to do. I trudged onward.

When I walked into the second grade classroom, I reached into my bag, guiltily scanning the room to see who was watching. I produced the yarn as Sister Mary Edna smiled and pulled out her gradebook to put the coveted checkmark by my name. And no one yelled out at me. Kids looked up but no one claimed the yarn as theirs.

Sister Mary Edna told me to "go put your yarn" in the basket at the back of the class, and this is where I was sure the aggrieved party would see their yarn in my hands. But again, nothing. After lunch, when it was time to begin our work on the art project—my image was a sunflower which needed green and yellow yarn—no one else grabbed "their green yarn" out of my hands. I finished my art project, and got an A.

At the end of that school day, as I walked home past the sad little tree fighting for life in the broken sidewalk where I found the yarn that morning, I thought about how the yarn came to be there, just waiting for me to pick it up. My yarn, saving me from the dreaded bad mark in the gradebook, a ball of yarn that, apparently, no one else in my class had dropped by mistake.

That ball of green yarn was put there for me, I realized then. My guardian angel was watching over me, giving me what I needed, protecting me from a bad grade. I knew this in an instant, intuitively, completely, beyond any doubt or otherwise rational thought.

It was not the last time my guardian angel delivered me from some awful outcome, pulled me back far from the edge of the cliff, saved me from myself or some wrong move, or pointed me in the right direction, when

I never even realized what she was doing at the time. My guardian angel is not like Santa Claus or the Easter bunny, the tooth fairy, or any other figment of fantasy or outright lies. She is a real and actual true person, who has kept her word my entire life and to this day.

There is no other way on earth to explain many of the bad things that could have happened but did not happen, or things that happened that have protected or saved me or given direction to my life. *I will watch over you always.*

In the Year of the Plague

I was dead, and see, I am alive forever and ever.

—*Rev 1:18*

I WILL WATCH OVER YOU *always.* Fast-forward to the now, to the knowledge of what "always" means. All the time, in all ways, every time; even when I don't realize that I am cared for, secure, protected. Even when it seems I am abandoned, forsaken, unloved.

Looking back on a lifetime of the mundane and the miraculous, the spectacular and the routine, on surprises and disappointments—I can see now, from this vantage point of time and perspective, how many times I have skirted so close to the edge, so close to the cliff, eluded imminent disaster, or wandered unaware into amazing serendipity, into changes for the better that I never could have anticipated nor planned.

I survived a near-fatal assault on my body by COVID, the plague of modern times, which took hold of me and would not let go for five frightening weeks. This was in the days before the vaccine, in the first year the plague struck humanity. When I arrived at St. Joseph's Hospital, the medical team in the emergency room was not hopeful. I had a runaway fever. My heartbeat fluctuated wildly out of control from low to high, from 50 to 130 beats and back down again. Blood pressure, likewise, could not be tamed. My blood oxygen level hovered just above eighty-five; below ninety-two is dangerous.

Out of ninety-six blood values they monitored over the course of my hospitalization, thirty-five of them were unsustainably too high or too low. During those weeks, I dropped over thirty pounds, almost twenty percent of my body mass.

After a week in the hospital, they put me in the intensive care unit, ready to be intubated at a moment's notice. I asked the nurses to take photos of me, in case these photos turned out to be my last. At night, the staff was never sure if I would make it till morning. I was oblivious to night and day, delirious and indifferent to the gravity of my plight. I had no reserves. Only hope.

As I lay in my bed five days in the intensive care unit, slowly losing ground day by day, hovering in the nether regions between anguish, despair, and all-consuming fear, I was always delicately conscious, like a light refreshing breeze on my face, of the nurses hovering over me, tending to me with constant IVs, blood draws, meds, and all manner of ministrations and care.

In those hours of delirium, at the edge of darkness and fatal depression, I came to see my nurses as little warbler birds, cooing and fluttering over me dispensing the treatment protocols with precision and great technical skill, but, more importantly, wrapping me in love—a gentle hand on my arm, a kind word in my ear, the manifestation of potent female nurturing care, the milk of human kindness.

The male nurses who cared for me were excellent as well. Capable. Efficient. Ever informative. But nothing in my life had prepared me for the absolute undeniable healing virtue of tender feminine energy. I don't remember all the nurses' names. But I will never forget the sweet hope they gave me in my darkest hours.

On my worst day in the intensive care unit, a team of three people came into my room—a hospital administrator with a clipboard in hand filled with forms, a social worker with the kindest eyes visible through her protective face shield, and the hospital chaplain. And ever so gently, like warm spring rain on a blossoming meadow, they began, in utmost kindness, a conversation with me about end-of-life issues.

They asked about my advance directive, confirmed my next of kin, asked if I felt love in my family and network. If I felt depressed. The delicacy with which this conversation was broached was unlike anything I had ever experienced.

They held my hand lovingly and brought me slowly, carefully to the edge of time. They stood with me there for a long moment of eternity. I lifted my eyes and looked across to the other side, and all my fears were vanquished. I felt restored to my rightful human dignity. I felt courage I never knew I had. And I saw this point not as an end but as the pinnacle of a life well lived, roundly experienced, and fully enjoyed. I smiled. I felt ready to meet my destiny, whatever came to be.

Then one morning, the crisis passed. The cytokine storm abated. I cannot attest to the specific reason it did, but I do know that the powerful force of prayers and love from my family and friends made calm the storm. I will always know this to be the case. My sister had all her "prayer warriors" in my corner. I know prayer works. And I know my guardian angel was ever by my side, ready to deliver me from the shadow of death and to my home, to the bosom of unconditional love.

> *Even though I walk through the darkest valley, I fear no evil; for you are with me; your rod and your staff—they comfort me. (Ps 23:4)*

After five weeks of illness and nineteen long, horrific nights in the hospital, I was well enough to be discharged. My near-fatal bout with the plague was a traumatic shock to my system and to my psyche that will echo deep within my consciousness for the rest of my life. Of this, I am sure. I think back on that time and I remember, like it was yesterday, every cup of coffee I had on each of those mornings that I woke up in my hospital bed—although *woke up* hardly seems like the proper term when there was never any real sleep to wake up from on those long and fearful nights.

I never got any sleep because the nurses came into my room every two hours round the clock, night and day, to inject a medication into my belly and to give me a dozen or more pills. Sleep—when it came—was fitful, more like a waking nightmare. There were times I was afraid to fall asleep, out of fear that I might never wake up.

And the word *remember* also hardly seems the proper word to use in this instance. Because I can remember every cup of coffee in the sense that I remember exactly how I felt with each new morning coffee each new morning, each new dawn, each new day that I "woke up" from the nightmare of COVID.

I remember the interminably long, slow hours on the big clock hanging on the wall directly in front of my bed; the hands of the clock hardly moving all night; the waiting, the interminable waiting; the occasional fitful sleep interrupted by another nurse, another bunch of meds, another midnight IV, another shot in the belly, another night of no sleep; and me just waiting.

Waiting till dawn to come again. Waiting to hold that tall paper cup of tepid thin coffee in my hand and sip. Sip. Sip slowly and deliberately. Sip the warm taste of something normal. Sip my morning cup of coffee in bed, like I used to do at home when life was normal.

The nurses saw this and understood me. Almost from the beginning, they made a point every morning of bringing me coffee from the nurses' station in the predawn hours long before the kitchen served up breakfast at nine.

Normal life for me in that hospital exists only in that cup that is now in my hands; the only normal I know is cradled warmly in my palms, as I lie on my back staring at the ceiling, taking another sip of normal, the way I have stared at so many other plain white ceilings in hotel rooms and in homes and in a hospital, where I am now, sipping that cup of coffee, waiting for dawn to flood through the window and fooling myself for a moment into believing that all is normal for just a solitary set of moments strung together to make a bit of normal in an abnormal world of COVID nights and COVID days, daydreaming, meandering in my head as far from this reality as I could for every waking moment.

And every moment the same questions. Will these be my last hours? Will I awaken once again tomorrow and peacefully sip that cup of normal? Or will tomorrow's cup sit unattended, full, there on the nightstand beside my bed; my waking nightmares over; my cold blue body wheeled down to the morgue; that cold white cup of normal left untouched; and nothing ever normal again after that?

> *Then he took a cup, and after giving thanks he gave it to them, saying, "Drink from it, all of you; for this is my blood of the covenant."* (Matt 26:27–28)

I have always valued my life, fully grateful for all the good that has come my way, but I never fully realized before I got sick that it was possible to value my death in the same manner. For in the solitary moments of my COVID despair, when death was near, I understood, deeply and with absolute clarity and peace of mind, just how rich and bountiful and happy my life has been. And with this revelation, I knew that death was a friend that I could love and embrace, as I have loved and embraced my life.

The English metaphysical poet John Donne accepted a close relationship with death throughout his life and his work. His poetry is filled with the understanding that death can wake us up to life. In his will, he left to a friend "the picture called The Skeleton which hangs in the hall." Donne knew that keeping death nearby can empower us to truly live.

In the Mexican tradition in which I was raised, death is both celebrated and embraced. The Nobel laureate Octavio Paz wrote in *The Labyrinth of Solitude*: "The word 'death' is not pronounced in New York, in Paris, in

London, because it burns the lips. . . . The Mexican, however, frequents it, jokes about it, caresses it, sleeps with it, celebrates it; it is one of his favorite toys and his most steadfast love." I have a small wooden skeleton work of folk art that I bought in Mexico decades ago, and a small luminescent skeleton in my bedroom that I can see glowing in the dark at night. I know that death is always just a halting breath away. This inspires me to live every hour fully when the new day dawns.

A few days after I was discharged from the hospital, Dr. Paul Shen, my physician at St. Joe's, called to see how I was doing. He told me I was lucky to come out of this alive, that, for all practical purposes, a man my age with all the problems COVID gave me should not have made it past day twelve. He told me there were three occasions when I was at the brink of death. My survival was quite amazing, he said. He told me my excellent conditioning saved me from certain death. But I believe it was music that saved my life.

I had my iPhone and charger with me all during my hospital ordeal. I listened to Spotify and YouTube Music constantly. I sang along to my old favorites all the time, hoping it would help me breathe easier. Hoping it would help me pass the time. Whistling past the graveyard, I suppose you could say.

There was a particular hymn I found on YouTube, a prayer in Latin from the Catholic Mass, that I remember from my days as an altar boy long ago in the barrio. It is the Agnus Dei, set to the music of Samuel Barber's *Adagio for Strings*. It is a beautiful, soulful, mournful melody, and it was one of my go-to treasures through many difficult moments. It made me cry. Crying helped me breathe and helped me feel alive again.

In those terrifying days and nights, music made for me all the difference between life and death. This, I know. And now that I have completed this memoir, I am on a trajectory to undertake my next life project—to master the piano and make my own music. I owe that much to my life and to the music that saved my life. What is that saying that is often, but mistakenly, attributed to C. S. Lewis? "You're never too old to set another goal or to dream a new dream." I hope for everyone that all your prayers are heard and answered, and that all your dreams come true.

Lamb of God, who takes away the sins of the world, hear our prayer.

When I was first admitted to the hospital, they conducted a functional assessment. A nurse asked me a lot of questions regarding my life habits. Did I exercise, and how much? Did I smoke, drink, do drugs?

What were my typical meals like? What was my state of mind? They were trying to determine risk and resiliency factors in my life, trying to run the calculus of my chances amid the implications of this new, poorly understood, life-threatening illness.

I remember thinking as I answered their questions that I owe a lot to my mom for the good homespun values of nutrition I learned from her and how I have always made the effort to eat the most nutritious food, avoid the junk, moderate my drinking, and exercise faithfully and often. I know this made a difference in my hour of need. My body was still strong and had a good running start at beating back this plague. I know this. My doctor realized this too. Thank you, Mom, for teaching me how to live, as well as how not to live, in equal measure. I don't hold the bad against you. You taught me enough of the good.

I am humbled and gratified to know that my survival was nothing short of miraculous. We don't often get the chance to see life through such a prism. The task now that I have set before myself is to discover the why of my deliverance. To what purpose am I here? Why was I allowed to live in the face of such catastrophic odds? What part fate? What part luck? What part destiny?

O Lord my God, I cried to you for help, and you have healed me.
(Ps 30:2)

Long-Term Care Insurance

In September 2020, four months before I came down with COVID, I decided to take out an insurance policy for long-term care insurance, which pays for the cost of hiring a home aide for up to twenty hours a week to cook meals, help with bathing, household chores, and errands—all the routine activities those in convalescence can't do for themselves. At the time, I figured I was older and vulnerable, single, without anyone who could do those things for me if I were laid up for any period of time. It was certainly not cheap but far less expensive than paying out of pocket. I figured, why not?—I might need it someday.

That someday came much sooner than I ever anticipated. In January 2021, I was struck down with the plague, and when I was discharged from the hospital in March, the first thing I did was call the long-term care insurance company. Within a day of my return home, I had an aide coming to my home four hours a day, five days a week, and her help was invaluable.

Over the course of the next five months during my rehabilitation, I got all the help I needed, and they were all very responsible, considerate, and good people. The bills I incurred for my long-term care ran into the tens of thousands of dollars. The insurance company made good on its responsibility and paid every last dollar on my claim. The amount of premium I had paid into the policy was less than two thousand dollars. It certainly was a gamble that paid off.

I was happy I had the foresight to purchase a long-term care insurance policy. But it has always been clear to me that the true long-term care insurance policy was my guardian angel—caring for me day and night, and saving me a lot of money in the process.

What Is Lost and What Is Gained

Today, I sit in my living room bathed in morning's golden light. And I remember how it was when I came home from the hospital. I remember it took me fifteen minutes to walk up the sixteen steps to my apartment. I remember how it fatigued me to walk the ten paces from my living room to the kitchen. I remember how I would take a few steps with my walker, sit on the sofa a few minutes, then get help standing up on my walker, then shuffle ten paces slowly back to the other chair. Someone had to hold on to my waist with a strap. Falling was deadly because of the blood thinners I was taking for the blood clots in my lungs that remained for a very long time.

We all have our profound hurts. I know many who have suffered more and are hurting far more than I ever did in my life. But, when I recall those days I almost died and what the plague did to my body, I find myself crying for a moment because I suffered so. I grieve my pain, my fear, my loss.

What I cry for is what I lost in my life. The whole month of February, isolated, alone, and uncertain of my path forward. I lost a good part of my body, withered away in atrophy after five bedridden weeks. I lost the easy "take it for granted" sense of breathing. I lost the energy to perform even the simplest physical task. I remember how it was, yes, but I do not remember out of a place of sorrow. I remember out of a place of love. I grieve the death of someone I once knew, that old Ray: a good man in his way but a man whose time had come. But I bear witness to the resurrection of life, of hope, and of love again.

> I long for the days when I could cry,
> cry because I felt like it, not because I had the time.
> Cry for sad, cry for joy, cry for love, cry for loss.
> Shed tears to the world to know that I'm alive
> not just cry in the lonely cell of my mind.
>
> —Ray Moisa, age fifteen

WHAT IS LOST AND WHAT IS GAINED

I lost so much, yes. But in the months I was recuperating from the plague, I did gain everything back and more. I lost much, but I found so much more. I found love, in so many subtle and profound ways. I found love at all levels, in all manifestations—love simple, love complicated, love for all people and creatures, love for self, love for every day that I can breathe, love for every night I can sleep without fear of never waking up.

It has not been a flawless journey to love. I have at times been that same, old, selfish, unkind, unthinking me. I have lashed out, stressed out, pouted, and sulked. Still. Yes, even still. And yet, each time I dig that hole of negative energy, I remember when I had not the energy to walk ten paces. Then it becomes easier to crawl out of that stupid hole of negativity I have dug for myself and ask for redemption, for forgiveness, as I move back to the light, back to the love again. I recalled the classics that I had studied during my years in Italy and what the ancients had to say about the right way to live and to love.

> *Love is patient; love is kind; love is not envious or boastful or arrogant or rude. It does not insist on its own way; it is not irritable or resentful; it does not rejoice in wrongdoing, but rejoices in the truth. It bears all things, believes all things, hopes all things, endures all things. (1 Cor 13:4–8)*

Italian Dawn

In the predawn light of a new day
untethered thoughts float to the surface—

a soft, warm sea of memory.
words struggle to find shape
in the land of unknowing,
but the only sound is a dog barking across the valley.

In the cobalt-dark sky outside my window
Venus hangs at the edge of a slivered moon,
in the glow of her light the trees cast shadows on the frosted grass.
in that solitary moment I realize you are gone,
were never here beside me.
Will never be again.

There is no pain more sharp
than the loss of love.
No deeper wound than a knife to the heart.
The edge of sadness lays bare all that came before,
and solitude stretches onward to the horizon like a lonely road to the sea.

Time beats in me like a pulse,
marking the quadrants of an empty chamber,
creating echoes that never end.
There will never be another moment like the ones we never shared,
There will never be laughter more insincere.
And in the days to come I see
only the blinding glare of hard, tarnished sunlight
obscuring all colors, melting shapes and form,
and I wait.

ITALIAN DAWN

Wait for the quiet, soothing respite of the night.
The submersion of all that I once believed I possessed
deep in the calming waters of sleep.
Wait for the frozen silvery moon and
Venus to cast the only light that illuminates all desire.

—Ray Moisa, on the end of his marriage and the beginning of a new life

The Parting of the Red Sea

IN THESE YEARS WHEN the human race has been locked in a death grip with COVID, our lives have been upended and flipped upside down. I have danced a bizarre duet with the plague, a strange relationship that goes back to the very first days this awful scourge has been visited upon our world. Even before I became infected, I was stalked by COVID.

When the plague first struck, I was visiting my friends in Italy, a family of olive oil producers living in the countryside an hour north of Rome. I like to call these people my Italian family, because I got to be very close to them, having rented a lovely little villa from them for more than two years after I retired.

I lived, worked, dined, and laughed with them. It was 2016, and I had decided to become an expat right after Donald Trump was elected. I was disgusted with the state of political affairs in America, and I had no desire to remain in this land that had elected Trump.

I had fallen in love with Italy after multiple vacations there over the years, and I had rented a lovely villa in my trips in prior years. It was achingly beautiful country, a land of ancient olive groves, fruit orchards, classic stone villages perched atop craggy mountaintops, and the world-famous Benedictine abbey of Farfa, constructed in the sixth century, and home to the oldest surviving manuscripts from the Dark Ages after the collapse of the Roman Empire.

I knew this beautiful, secluded villa well, and when I retired, I went there for an extended visit, and it was during this visit that Trump came to power. Within days after the election, I made my decision to apply for a permanent resident visa and move to Italy for good. I returned to the States, stored my larger possessions, and carried what I could back to Italy at the start of the new year. I lived in this beautiful villa fifty kilometers north of Rome and began a life that I can now see was simply too good to last.

It was a glorious time that seems like a dream to me now. I lived like a child, free of all care, uncaring of time and a stranger to obligation. By day, I studied the classics of ancient Rome and Greece—Ovid, Seneca, Euripides, Plato, Petronius, Plutarch, Cicero, Homer, Lucretius, Augustine—searching the wisdom of the ages for clues on how to live the contemplative life and how to love in the right way.

I loved to walk the short distance to the abbey of Farfa. The route took me from the hill where my villa had a commanding view, down to a narrow, lush valley below. The Farfa River meandered through this valley, and it was in this place, where I crossed a narrow wooden bridge over the water, that a man by the name of Giovanni di Pietro di Bernardone, who became known to us as St. Francis of Assisi, had stopped here almost nine hundred years ago on his sojourn to Rome fifty kilometers away. Bernardone rested here for the afternoon before walking up the steep hill on the other side of the river, to stay at the abbey with the monks for a few days of fasting and meditation, before continuing on for the final day's journey to Rome.

Francis of Assisi made this pilgrimage to Rome to chastise Pope Innocent III and the cardinals of the Holy See for their obscene wealth, venality, and greed, when there were so many poor people in Christendom struggling to put a scrap of food on the table. He admonished them to renounce their vast worldly possessions and their decadent ways and become more like Christ.

Francis must have had his own powerful guardian angel protecting him, because he was never excommunicated for standing up to those powerful "princes of the church." In fact, the pope granted Francis all his requests over the years to form several religious orders for men and women. And only two years after his death, Francis was canonized a saint.

On Sunday mornings, I would attend the traditional Mass at the abbey. This Mass offered Gregorian chant, which soothes my soul deeply for reasons I can describe only as primal, in that indefinable and magical way that only music, the *lingua bella* of the soul, can do.

This traditional music of the church, Gregorian chant, takes me back to my childhood, to a time of innocence, wonder and delight. To a time when I believed not only in my guardian angel and in God but in the institution of the church as the true house of God. As my belief in my guardian angel and God became only more profound over time, my faith in the Roman Catholic Church was destroyed as the hypocrisy and mendacity of the church became more apparent, the more I saw.

> *Why are you cast down, O my soul, and why are you disquieted within me? Hope in God; for I shall again praise him, my help and my God. (Ps 43:5)*

In the evenings, my Italian family and I discussed world politics and the olive oil harvest while eating fine Italian cuisine prepared from recipes handed down through their family for generations. Occasionally, I took the train into Rome for a taste of city life, but, for the most part, I wanted the solitude and seclusion of a monk's life, reading, taking long walks in the countryside, regenerating a new me.

My Italian family owned and leased in the area substantial groves of olives and harvested them for the production of organic extra virgin olive oil. I took an active interest in the work of the farm, happy to help with manual labor in every change of the seasons—pruning the trees (*la potatura*) in the dead of winter; in the spring, we foraged in the fields and forests for wild asparagus, chicory, mushrooms, borage, wild fennel, anise, wild cherries, blackberries, strawberries, and blueberries. The summers were too hot to do much more than lie inside my cool stone villa in the heat of the day, read literature, and practice my Italian.

My favorite time of year by far was autumn, especially the months of October and November. This was the time for *la raccolta*, the harvest, when extra day laborers were hired from the nearby villages to shake the olive trees of their fruit, which were collected in large nets spread out on the ground around the ancient trees, in a tradition of manual labor that has not changed in millennia. The nets were then scooped up and the olives dumped into a small pickup truck that raced back to the small family mill where the rest of us were eagerly waiting.

For maximum quality preservation, the olives need to be pressed within three hours of harvesting, so every minute it took to drive them from the nearby groves to the mill was crucial. From there, the olives were hurriedly scooped into large plastic crates just heavy enough for a strong man to lift and carry from one station to another. The olives were then separated from the small branches and twigs that held them to the tree, and olives that were noticeably bad at this point were immediately tossed into the compost bin. All this was done as quickly and efficiently as we could.

The olives were then weighed on a large farm scale, equipment that was very old school, yet extremely reliable to the gram. I know this for a fact, because one evening I tested the accuracy of this scale, which was big enough for two men to stand on, by laying a five-kilogram bag of flour on it. Not one gram off. I was amazed.

After recording the weight of the olives at this stage of the process, the olives were then poured into a shaker, which was a simple sluice-like piece of equipment run by a small electric motor that was turned on and that then lightly shook the olives down the metal slope through a chute and out into another crate to be hauled to the mill, the final stage in the process. As the sluice vibrated, the olives moved little by little down to the exit point and into the crate below.

Two people stand opposite each other at the shaker and pick out the bad olives one by one as they vibrate down the chute. Again, manual labor that a machine can never replace. This was the job I loved to do.

I was taught what to look for in an olive that had gone bad. Some were bad from too much rain or not enough rain. Some had the telltale holes of the dreaded olive worm, which got embedded by a wasp into the olive early in the growing season; then the worm became a larva and ate out the meat of the fruit.

These imperfections degraded the quality of the olive, and you could taste a bad batch of olive oil and tell what its problem came from. I learned how to discern bad oil. I was chosen to be the guy in charge of quality control because I am a bit of a perfectionist, and I got very good at quickly tossing out the bad olives. When we were done with a truckload of olives and waiting for the arrival of the next load, I would wander through all the crates of cleaned olives and search out the bad ones that we had missed.

My attention to detail was commended by everyone. I was designated the *Accendino* or Fire Starter which gave me the "privilege" of flipping on the switch on the electric shaker. I always did this with a huge dramatic flourish, which made everyone laugh. They loved me for the dedication and energy the *Americano* brought to the effort. I loved them all back.

After cleaning the olives, I helped pour the full crates of olives into the mill, which pressed them into oil. This took many hours, and Frank, the man who was responsible for this stage, often worked into the wee hours of the morning while the press processed the thousands of kilograms of olives into hundreds of liters of extra virgin olive oil. Frank had to constantly make adjustments to the mix, letting out a little oil now and then to taste it. He was an expert at this.

I would often stay late into the night with Frank, the *frontoiano*: the man in charge of running the mill. I would pick through the crates of olives one last time, tossing out the few remaining bad ones before they went to press. Everyone would be gone to bed but we two.

As the mill slowly turned the olives to mush, then to a thick, viscous oil, Frank and I would stand outside the millhouse, out on the loading dock facing the eastern expanse of the Italian night. We would listen to the sounds of the night coming up from the valley below us, and he would tell me the names of the animals we heard talking with each other.

"*Volpe*," he would tell me as the fox shrieked its frightening call. "*Lupo*," he would say when we heard a wolf's baleful cry. "*Ci sono lupi in questo posto, Francesco?*" Are there wolves here, Frank? "*Si*," he would tell me. "*Alcuni.*" A few.

Frank took another long drag from his cigarette, and I turned up my collar against the chilly predawn air. We looked to the east, where Venus dangled under the fingernail moon in a cobalt sky, as bright as a diamond, as precious as hope. I felt alive in this place. Like Adam in the first dawn of man.

The pressing of the olives was reminiscent of the traditional barefoot stomping of grapes that we associate with romantic Italian farm life in making wine. The entire family was involved in the work—my friends' parents and siblings and uncle and aunt, as well as friends from Rome who would drop by now and then on the weekends—whoever was willing to come by for a few hours or a few days to enjoy the lovely, warm autumn afternoons of golden light in the Italian countryside, wine pouring freely for all, mountains of pasta carbonara or pasta alla Norma at lunchtime, and plenty of fun and joking all day long. It seemed like a dream, it was so like a fairytale and yet so genuine.

I was a character of great interest to all in this circle of my Italian family and friends. The old American expatriate who turned his back on a sweet life in San Francisco to start anew. I was told that I was *molto corragioso*—very courageous—for embarking on such a challenging adventure at my age.

They laughed at the fact that here was a man who reversed the flow of immigration from the new country back to the old. Some people shook their heads in disbelief. Many Italians wanted to leave this land of infernal political dysfunction, poor economic opportunity, and many backward traditions that people clung to for no good reason. But I knew deep inside that I was the one who had come to the good life.

I soon proved my worth beyond a doubt to everyone. The first year I helped with *la raccolta*, we entered our olive oil in an international organic olive oil competition in the south of Italy. These competitions consisted of a blind tasting by expert olive oil tasters. Our oil won a gold medal in our class, out of hundreds of bottles submitted. We were stunned and elated. My Italian family had never won a gold medal before, and we piled into the car and headed south on a clear, crisp late winter day to receive our medal and certificate.

Thrilled by this great achievement, we submitted bottles to an international competition in Spain, a country also known for its excellent olive oil. We won gold there as well. We flew to Spain to receive our award and to revel in the joy that we deserved so much. I was high with excitement.

The following year, we poured our hearts into the *raccolta* and produced an olive oil that everyone in the community, near and far, hailed as superlative. This time, we submitted samples to two of the most important international competitions in the world—the New York International Olive Oil Competition in New York City, and the Los Angeles International Extra Virgin Olive Oil Competition. Again, we took gold medals in each. I knew I was now a "made man" in the family. I thought I could live like this forever. It was a dream come true.

Things did not work out as I had dreamed they would, however. I came to realize on a day-to-day basis how difficult it was to adjust to a different culture at my age, to keep up with the language, to miss my family and my long-time friends. I had a small medical setback there, and it began to dawn on me how things might be if I were ever hospitalized in this foreign country.

The medical care was top notch and free, of course. I had no concerns over the quality of treatment I would receive. But I wondered: how would I feel in a hospital with no one to speak English to, no one in my family or close circle of American friends to visit me?

After more than two years living this idyllic life, I decided I had to return home. I realized that I had succumbed to a romanticized vision of life in Italy. Indeed, I had lived a romanticized vision of life. But in the harsh light of day, under the wilting Italian summer sun, the dream slowly began to fade to reality. As the saying goes, planning is what we do, but life is what happens. I took the memories of my beautiful Italian life, carefully wrapped them up and packed them in my suitcases, and made the long, lonely, dispiriting trip back home.

I stayed awake the entire fifteen-hour trip back to America. I had a long conversation with my guardian angel, thanking her for staying with me throughout this epic period in my life, keeping watch over me, and guiding me always, always toward only the best this world had to offer. I got what I had come for. And that should be enough for any man. I heard my guardian angel's calming words in the steady hum of the jet engines at 36,000 feet: *Ray, I have always watched over you.*

So I returned to the States in the fall of 2018 and spent a few months in San Francisco, my former home, where I got reacquainted with my dear friends and worked as a volunteer getting out the vote for Democratic candidates in the 2018 midterm elections. It was good to feel that I was doing something meaningful to help turn back the tide of right-wing, neo-fascist Republican hegemony in Washington. It was gratifying to see that our work paid off with a tsunami of Democratic voters who flipped the power dynamic and brought about the much-needed change of direction in Congress.

After completing my work on the electoral phone banks that fall, I moved to Eureka to be close to my family and set about to make a new life for myself at home in the States.

I now look back fondly on those years in Italy and on making gold-medal oil. I know I was not the only one who worked hard for that oil. And I know it is the mark of hubris to believe that I made a difference. But the family never won gold for their oil before I came, and they have never won gold in the years since I left. I will never forget those four gold medals in two years. For me, I do take pride in what I contributed to that amazing feat, because I know I gave it my all. And, in the end, this is all that matters in any endeavor we undertake.

One year later, I returned for a three-month visit to my Italian family, arriving just before New Year's Eve 2019, so that I could enjoy the spectacular celebration of *Capodanno* (New Year's Eve) that Italians go all out for—an epicurean and bacchanalian feast lasting long into the night and featuring some of the finest gourmet dishes the Italians are rightly famous for.

I like to recall that it was a party of nine hours, eight courses of food, seven bottles of wine, six people, five desserts, four bottles of prosecco, three cats, two cups of coffee, all in one hell of a party. And zero hangovers! *Capodanno* is a feast that is not to be missed, and I was grateful to be there for it and a little sad as I was reminded of the life I had to give up for many practical reasons. But a three-month visit was enough at this point, I figured, and so I eased myself back into the routine—albeit temporarily—that I had come to cherish in my *dolce vita* years.

Fate, once again, would have its way, of course. For it was during this three-month visit to Italy that COVID first emerged in Wuhan, then quickly made its way by mid-January to the north of Italy, to Milan and environs, to be exact, a focal point of business where the Chinese had been investing for years on "road-and-bridge" infrastructure projects in Italy. From there, the rest is history, as they say. The plague quickly began to devastate the Italian population, for all the reasons that are by now painfully well documented.

Within a month after my arrival in Italy for *Capodanno*, the plague was ravaging the northern province of Bergamo, which was populated mostly by older people still living in the ancient villages where they were born. The region is close to Milan, the industrial, technical, and business hub of Italy, the home of many younger, white-collar professionals. A lot of those residents would often travel the short distance to Bergamo on the weekends to visit their parents and grandparents.

The uncontrollable firestorm of plague had a devastating impact on all of us living in Italy, and we clung to the news daily, trying to make sense of the devastation that was chronicled in the media. But for us, my Italian family and me, life continued in a somewhat normal fashion. For we were living in rural isolation, on a farm more than a mile away from the nearest ancient village and an hour by train from Rome.

We had a garden that produced veggies even in winter, and we foraged some greens as a matter of custom in the woods around us. Local farmers produced some of the protein we bought, and Francesco and Chiara, my two family members living on the farm near me, made the biweekly trek to the market for everything else we consumed.

And, of course, we always had plenty of organic extra virgin olive oil that was produced on the farm and that Italians consume daily, so our exposure to the plague was almost nil, and we did not ever feel personally at risk. Despite the ravaging effects of the plague, I felt safely wrapped in an insulated cocoon, like the characters in Boccaccio's thirteenth-century tale of the Black Death, *The Decameron*.

In *The Decameron*, a group of ten young people leave their homes in Florence for a villa in the countryside to escape the Black Death that is ravaging cities all over Europe and the known world. They tell stories to each other every night, stories about love and life lessons. It is a masterpiece of classical early Italian prose and stands up well to this day. My friends and I were safe in our countryside retreat, and we kept ourselves occupied with life as normal.

The story, however, was much different on the other side of the Atlantic back home with my family. Of course, they also were watching the awful news and they were desperate and panicked imagining me in the crosshairs of imminent doom. They could not comprehend that I was, in fact, living in the eye of the storm rather than in the crosshairs of a weapon of mass destruction.

Except for the news reports that we monitored daily, life for me in my sweet little villa was normal and calm and free of stress in almost every other way. Although I had planned to take some trips during my three-month visit, as I had often done in the past throughout Italy and other cities in Europe, I was, nevertheless, content to stay on the farm with my kitty, Broccoloncini, whom I had missed dearly, and she and I would take long walks in the countryside together.

I was safe as long as I stayed in our little corner of paradise. I needed nothing more during those months. I was living comfortably in wonderful delusional seclusion like the characters in *The Decameron*.

Jo Ann, however, became more panicked the longer I stayed and the worse the news became, but I was determined to remain until the date on my return ticket, which was March 16. I had, over the years, become accustomed to flying first class, especially on long transatlantic flights. I had the resources to do so, and it was so much more comfortable for someone who loves to travel as much as I do. To change my plans was excessively expensive. I was safe and felt no compelling reason to get out of Italy. So I decided to wait it out. How long could this possibly last? Surely, it would be over soon. But my sister could not see my logic.

So the plague did last longer than I thought it would. I recall vividly her phone call to me when Trump announced on March 14 that he was sealing off the borders in two days to all incoming travelers. She was almost hysterical, and I suppose I could not blame her. She was yelling at me: "Come home, Ray!" She was afraid that, with the borders closed, I might get stuck in Italy, which, to me, actually, was not the worst possible outcome.

My sister had recently lost her daughter to cancer, which had progressed from diagnosis to death in less than six weeks. Nine months after her daughter passed, her husband had died in a motorcycle accident. So I understood that she was not in the best place emotionally, still grieving and still prone to worry about everyone else in the family. She and I had always been the closest of siblings, and we both cared for each other deeply. But I dug in and was not to be persuaded.

As it turned out, my confidence in my judgment and my situation turned out to be wholly justified—and rewarded. For when Trump closed the borders, it caused widespread panic among Americans in foreign lands. Tens of thousands of people rushed to the airlines online and in ticket offices to try to book flights back to the States in the one day remaining before the order took effect.

The next day, March 15, all the international airports in the U.S. were overwhelmed with hordes of incoming American travelers entering the country. Tens of thousands of panicked people at every major airport stood in line for hours and hours processing through customs, at baggage claim, and everywhere else. The television news showed the images of a tide of humanity that had descended on the airports. The system collapsed under the weight of so many people at ticket counters and at customs stations converging all at once.

People paid dearly, financially and emotionally, to get home within that short, twenty-four-hour window before it shut for who knows how long. But I refused to panic. I felt everything would work out fine, even if I got "stuck" in Italy.

But Trump's order was poorly crafted—big surprise—and people assumed that everyone would be barred from entering the country. As it turned out, within twenty-four hours the U.S. State Department issued a clarification. All American travelers would be allowed reentry to the U.S. The ban applied only to foreigners.

So on March 16, the day after the panicked descent on our airports of a crushing torrent of travelers, I packed my bags, took the train, which was completely empty, from our nearby village to Fiumicino Airport in Rome, to board my flight home, on the date of my original itinerary. The conductor and I were alone on the train, so we spent the hour talking (masked and socially distanced) as we passed along the route through empty train stations.

I arrived at the airport hotel in the terminal to stay overnight for my early morning flight, and the hotel was empty except for all the maids busy cleaning with antiseptic every available surface. I stayed in a room that I was assured no one had occupied for many weeks since the plague began.

The flight home, too, had a few passengers in economy and no one but me in first class. The flight crew treated me royally, and I enjoyed every convenience possible, talking with the flight attendants, practicing my Italian on them. When I arrived from my nonstop flight to Los Angeles, the airport also was deserted, as was the shuttle to my airport hotel. The hotel at LAX also was empty. I have never experienced such an empty everything in travel.

I felt like Moses with the Red Sea parting before the Israelites, allowing them passage to the promised land safe from the armies of Pharoah. Indeed, my last name, Moisa, is said to be derivative of the name Moses. So be it, and so it is with my covenant with my guardian angel.

I felt, then and now, that my determination to stick to my original itinerary on my return flight home was not stubbornness or a cocky sense of swagger and defiance of the odds. The honest emotion I felt was, first, that I was safest staying in place there in my villa, self-quarantined under optimal, protected conditions. I also felt, like much of the rest of the world, that the plague could very well be under control by the time I returned home, almost two months after it began to sweep across the world from China and Italy. How wrong we all were about that.

When Trump issued his order closing off the country, I did try for a while to change my ticket online, but the websites were jammed and continuously crashed under the burden of so many desperately trying to get through.

In my daily meditation at the time, I prayed for peace, for myself and the world, and for the right outcome for me. Then, I gave myself over to God's plan, trusting that everything would work out, no matter what happened. As it turned out, the result was the best possible outcome for me and, I feel, a direct consequence of my firm belief that everything would work out fine, even when it isn't clear what in the world is going on.

Faith, I suppose you would call it. I was ready to face my destiny, whatever came to be. *I will watch over you always*—words I took to heart, words I always believed, words that never seemed to fail me.

> *Know that I am with you and will keep you wherever you go, and will bring you back to this land; for I will not leave you until I have done what I have promised you. (Gen 28:15)*

dancing with a stranger

in the long and languid summer evenings
when i taught you how to dance salsa
on the veranda of my villa
under a twinkling Italian sky,

holding gently to the moment,
moving slowly to the beat,
leaning into tempo,
listening to you breathe,
then releasing you back to the arms of the man you love,

our movements were choreographed by fate,
destined to never be.
we held time and tempo in our arms—
fragile, fleeting, as ephemeral
as the mournful song of the nightjar in the still air,
as distant as the stars above.

it could never be love, only the shadow at our feet cast by the moonlight.
you laughed, and my loneliness cut me to the bone.

Lockdown

On the day I arrived home after my three-month return visit to Italy in the winter of 2020, California's Governor Newsom issued a mandatory fourteen-day lockdown throughout the state as the plague was raging across America. I was already obligated by law to go into fourteen-day quarantine after coming in from Europe. My sister back home in Eureka knew this, and she had already filled my apartment cupboards and refrigerator with enough food and staples to last for more than a few weeks.

And so my life in isolation began. I was prepared to live without human contact for the next two weeks, a hermit in seclusion, as was much of the rest of the state. I stayed indoors most of the time, reading, on the phone with friends, listening to music or watching television, except for my daily power walk to get some sunshine and fresh air.

There has been much research about the harmful effects of the COVID isolation we endured in our attempts to contain the plague and prevent its spread. Lockdowns, quarantines, self-isolation, the shuttering of schools, workplaces, and public venues where people gather for all manner of social activities like theaters, sports arenas, community meeting halls, and auditoriums, as well as hospitals, where patients no longer are allowed to receive visitors.

Everywhere in society, in every nation on the planet, it's as if each of us has been a prisoner in solitary confinement. The serious damage to our sense of well-being, social creatures that we are, has been immeasurable and real for everyone, from the youngest children in school, to the elderly in long-term care homes, and everyone in between. The long-term effects will be felt for a generation or more, I am sure. People are just not made to live like hermits in isolation for long periods of time. It goes against our nature.

Living without normal human contact like that was, without a doubt, a very difficult situation to tolerate. We all know this from our experiences with life in quarantine. We need social interaction with others like we need sunshine and fresh air.

During my quarantine period, I spent a lot of time thinking about this. At some point in isolation, ancient memories began to emerge from deep within my psyche. The lines between my conscious and subconscious states began to blur and merge, and I found myself going deep within and recalling things long buried in my past.

Flashback to a state of being, to a place in the deep subconscious, to a time before there was being, to the time before I was born. My mother and father had split up shortly after I was conceived, and my father was never really in my life, except for a few notable occasions now and then when I was older. My mother already had a four-year-old boy, Sonny, and no means of support. She was a welfare mom at the age of twenty-two with another mouth on the way—me in her belly.

So before I was born, my mom made the decision to give me up for adoption. She told her doctor she wanted them to take me away as soon as I came out of her womb. She didn't even want to see me. At least she knew that to see me would be too painful for her. So my fate as a motherless child was fixed even before I began my life, and they snatched me away the moment I emerged. I never suckled at her breast. I never smelled her warmth. I never bonded with my mother. They put me in the bassinet in the nursery, and from there I went off to a foundling hospital.

Of course, I have no idea what those first days and months of my infant life were like. There are no cute baby pictures, no mommy and daddy memories, no anecdotes about who I looked like when I was a newborn. The historical record is a blank. My infancy does not exist in anyone's memory.

But if you asked me to think hard about it, if I were under hypnosis, for example, I would imagine that my protomemory is of extreme and deleterious isolation, of having no loving mother or father to hold me close and love me as an infant needs to be loved and held as only a parent can do.

I would have to say in my protomemory state that I certainly did not get mother's milk, and no doubt had only formula from a bottle. I would tell you, if you asked me to go deep into protomemory, that this little infant boy was probably left to cry alone a lot in his bassinet in the foundling hospital, a case of not enough caregivers for too many babies.

I would have to say, and I have felt this keenly from my earliest memories, that I felt abandoned, unloved, and left to my own wits to survive a cruel and heartless world, a motherless, fatherless child from the moment of birth.

Living under quarantine, cut off from all personal human contact, the feeling was as I imagined it must have felt for me in the first six months of my life. Primordial feelings of isolation and abandonment echoed with every heartbeat as I lay in the couch in my small apartment. This unnatural state of being alone without human touch, without a human smile, without other eyes to look into, took me far back and deep into a past I could not possibly truly remember, and yet, somehow, a part of me does remember the great sense of loss and loneliness of a little boy-child too young to know what has happened and what it is that is missing from his young life.

Flashback to a state of being, to a place in deep subconscious, a time before there was being, the time before I was born. I will watch over you always.

It occurred to me as these thoughts of isolation, loneliness, and abandonment began to filter up through my consciousness that perhaps my guardian angel has been such a strong and active and known presence in my life because she was assigned to protect this innocent baby left to fend for himself by unfeeling parents. She came to watch over me, to protect me, to be the mother and father I didn't have. Again, I am reminded of Holy Scripture.

> *Look at the birds of the air; they neither sow nor reap nor gather into barns, and yet your heavenly Father feeds them. Are you not of more value than they? (Matt 6:26)*

Six months or so after I was born, my mother had a change of heart and went searching for me and took me back with her. Then, one afternoon when I was thirteen years old, my mother, in a tequila-fueled drunken outpouring of guilt and remorse, revealed to me the story of my birth. And that story, in and of itself, became another traumatic episode for me and created yet other complications and stress for a sensitive kid at the cusp of adolescence trying to make sense of the world.

I remember thinking then that her revelation helped explain a lot of things that were wrong about our relationship. For, although Mom may have done the brave thing, the right thing, by taking me back into her life, she was never a kind and loving mother. She behaved to me like she regretted her decision to take me back with her. Growing up, I never felt much love from her.

She had a very short fuse if I ever behaved in a less than perfect manner. She was often abusive and impatient with me. I came to realize as I got older that she never fully reconciled her inability to cope with being a single mom on welfare, and no doubt suffered a profound sense of failure and guilt for the way she had initially abandoned me in those formative first six months of my life.

I always felt pressure to excel at being "the perfect son" in order to win her approval and affection. This constant state of anxiety and hypersensitivity to her moods caused me a lot of stress in my childhood.

On the other hand, I can see now that, in many ways, this constant desire to please, to excel, to be the best child to avoid her wrath, has actually enabled me to succeed in school and career, forcing me to constantly push myself to do better, to be better, to please my teachers and my employers. I became a straight-A student in school and a successful professional in my career.

In this way, I have to say that I owe my success to Mom. I also acknowledge and credit my mom for her difficult decision to take me back, despite the hardships she faced in raising three kids without a father. It was tough living on welfare in the projects. I know she did the best she could at the time. I believe she gave me up for adoption hoping I would have a better life in a caring, loving, secure home.

Still, I have always felt that she often took out her frustrations on me over the poor choices she had made in her life and that she treated me harshly when I needed kindness and caring.

I am sure my mom once had dreams of her own, and her own childhood was not easy either. This, I understand. So the cycles of intergenerational poverty and abuse, the language that is today in the common vocabulary and so well understood by child psychologists and social scientists, played out in our relationship to a degree that traumatized me and caused deep psychological problems that I still struggle to address.

And yet, I can see that this trauma, in its own way, propelled me to overcome the poverty that I was born into and to break free of the barrio.

I am glad that I was able to rise above the fray and break the cycle of trauma to excel in school and then become a successful professional in a challenging career. Poverty, abuse, parental abandonment (not once but multiple times, in fact) were real and psychological hurdles that I was fortunate enough to figure out how to leap over and to land on my feet.

I know that I am a better person, not despite the traumas I suffered in my childhood but because of them. So I thank my mom for doing her best, while I must acknowledge the stress I suffered because of her. In life, there are risk factors and there are resiliency factors, and sometimes, the two can be one and the same, depending on the individual.

And I will always know that my guardian angel was there for me at every turn and always had my back, pushing me to do the right thing in school and work and, certainly, protecting the innocent baby without a mom for six months, without a father for life. *I will watch over you always. Remember the lilies of the field.*

I must have been a constant and painful reminder to my mom of the trauma she had inflicted on me by abandoning me at birth. She has been honest in telling me that I had a lot of developmental problems when she brought me home. I did not perform according to the usual benchmarks of early childhood development that parents and pediatricians look for as the baby grows. The simple things: lifting my head, crawling, shuffling, standing up, walking, talking. I had problems that were evident as soon as she brought me home. She took me to the doctor, but he could find no physical impediments. She admits fearing that I was damaged goods.

Child development research conducted in the 1940s shows that infants in foundling hospitals failed to thrive after having been abandoned by their mothers. Depression and a host of developmental problems were evident in these infants, traumatized at a very early age by abandonment.

One anecdote that Mom has told me illustrates both the problems I manifested as well as her painful response to them. I never spoke one intelligible word until I was five years old. Instead, I grunted like a little animal.

My mother took me to the doctor one day to see if I had a physical problem that prevented me from speaking normally. The doctor found nothing physically wrong. He told her: "Well, maybe he just has nothing to say." This seems funny now, but, as it turns out, it was actually quite revealing about my state of mind.

It had become a "thing" among my aunts and uncles to see who could be the first person to coax me to talk. One day, when I was five, an uncle came to visit. As he was getting ready to leave, he came over to me to chat me up one last time and try to get me to say something, as was the custom. My mom, frustrated by my recalcitrance, threw up her arms and said to my uncle: "Oh, just leave him alone, he's stupid."

After my uncle was gone, I went up to my mom and said to her, calmly and in perfect English: "I'm not stupid, Mommy. Why did you say that?" Mom was both elated to realize I could speak and also devastated that I had understood what she had said. These were the first words ever out of my mouth. From that moment on, I proved to be an articulate little chatterbox with a fully developed vocabulary, although silent for years—keeping my own counsel, watching, waiting, and always thinking.

In first grade at Resurrection School, I brought home my first report card filled with As in every subject. When my mom saw my report card she could not believe it. She grabbed me by the hand and immediately marched with me back to school. She went to my first grade teacher, Sister Mary Gilberta, and told the nun that she must have made some mistake. I was not a very smart kid, Mom told the nun. Perhaps I got the grades that belonged to another student.

Sister Mary Gilberta told her, "Oh no, your son is a very bright student, the best one in the class." She took out her gradebook and showed my mom all the assignments with As for each one. Mom was shocked to discover that I was not as stupid as she thought I was. That I was, in fact, a smart little boy. I went on continuing to be a straight-A student throughout grammar school, then high school, and, eventually, college.

I loved school from the very beginning, obviously, and I excelled in that environment. I have come to believe that I was such a good student because I was in an environment where I had an opportunity to shine, to prove myself and my worth without any preconceived notions that I was stupid. I believe that I was fully aware on a subconscious level that my mother (and my father) never valued me for who I was. So I would find someone who did. And I did. In school, I had a chance to start out with a clean slate, a level playing field, free of the handicap of being made to feel as I did at home: a burden to my mom. I felt appreciated in school. I felt my talents were recognized. I responded to the positive feedback that I never got from my mother. In fact, I craved it, and in return, I proved that I was worthy of caring.

In school, away from the harsh, disapproving eyes of my unappreciative mother, I was able to present "the real me" and be accepted by approving, supportive, and kind mother figures, the nuns. I had internalized the understanding that my mother did not want me and could not accept me, so I would seek acceptance by the outside world, and enjoy the rewards the world had to offer, since my mother clearly had no faith in me. "I'll show her" was the silent, subconscious mantra of my childhood years. This understanding, it turns out, has served me well.

My guardian angel protected me from harm, but she also pushed me in the right direction, toward the places that would do me the most good.

As a child, school was the first arena for my self-realization, my self-fulfillment to occur. And I not only survived, but I thrived against all the odds, in the projects, where dreams die young.

Dad

Flashback to a state of being, to a place in deep subconscious, to a time before there was being, to the time before I was born. I will watch over you always.

My father was never around much, after disappearing for the first few years of my life. I knew very little about the man, only that he was a mestizo of Navajo, other Native, and Mexican American lineage. On our birthdays or at Easter now and then he would call my mom and arrange to pick us up and take us to his mother's house across town. I am sure his mother, my grandmother, ragged on him constantly to be more active in our lives, and this once- or twice-a-year event was his way of appeasing her desire to see us, her first grandchildren, as well as his own sense of paternal obligation. He was more like a stranger to me for much of my childhood, though.

Most times, Dad never showed up, while Sonny and I sat, dressed in our Sunday best, outside our front door in the projects, waiting and waiting for hours, looking up anxiously when a car drove by on Hunter Street, disappointed once again when it kept going past our section of grey cinder block apartments.

Sonny would beg Mom to call Dad to ask when he was coming for us, and we could always tell by her tone and her responses on the phone that Dad was too drunk to bother. At times like this, Sonny would get quiet and turn inward and sulk away. I would go inside to change my clothes and then play with Jo Ann, who has always been my best friend throughout our lives.

To the time before I was born. My dad took up with another woman when I was still in my mother's womb. My dad and this other woman had a son, Alex, born five months after me. Alex looked very much like me but with green eyes to my hazel ones. But beyond the physical, our resemblance ends.

I got to know Alex somewhat as I grew older, at Grandma's house when Dad would have us kids there all together once or twice a year (on those days when he actually came for us) and then later, in my adolescence when I was actively trying to form a connection to him, to my father, and to the relatives I had never really known as I was growing up.

On those rare occasions as a little boy when my dad did arrive to take Sonny and me to Grandma's house, it was always very traumatic and frightening for me. The scene usually went like this. Dad would come, finally, hours after the appointed time. He and Mom would argue a bit as she would initially refuse to let us go because he had been drinking. Mom would finally give in, since she felt we ought to get to be with our father, even if he was drunk. I suppose her logic was that a drunk dad was better than no dad at all. At that time, drunk driving did not seem to carry quite the stigma that it does today. Crazy, I know. The first stop before Grandma's house was the bar on Whittier Boulevard where Dad's bookie hung out. Dad would leave Sonny and me in the back seat, while he went inside, "for just a little while, boys," he would tell us and dash in. Dad loved betting on the horses, at Santa Anita or Hollywood Park. It didn't matter where, he was always looking for his big win and always losing his paycheck to the horses. Forty or so minutes later, Dad would return to the car, more inebriated than before, and either happy or sulking, depending on his luck at the track that day.

When we arrived at Grandma's house, the scene was always one of total drunken noisy chaos, of music way too loud; heavy cigarette smoke hanging in the air; kids running in and out of the house, some laughing, some crying; grown-ups falling all over themselves, grown-ups with drinks in hand fighting with one another, or grown-ups in a bedroom shooting up heroin behind closed doors.

I remember on one occasion in Grandma's house I opened a bedroom door looking for the bathroom. I saw an uncle on the bed turning blue in the face, the belt still wrapped around his arm, while the others around him were smacking his face, thumping his chest, trying to revive him, and someone was yelling at me to "shut the fucking door!" I must have been around seven or eight years old. I remember this moment like it was yesterday. I will never forget it as long as I live.

I never liked these visits to Grandma's. She was okay, a grandma who doted on us kids for the first ten minutes after we arrived, then slipping away into her bedroom to watch her telenovelas while her progeny caused havoc in her small, cramped home. Everything about these visits to Grandma's frightened me.

I was only a little boy, but I could sense that Sonny and I were there to kill two of Dad's birds with one stone: to appease his warped sense of paternal obligation and to satisfy his mother's desire to see her grandchildren, if only for a brief time once or twice a year.

But these visits were never about us or what we hoped to gain or needed from spending time with our father. The energy in the house, with people I hardly knew—cousins, aunts, and uncles I saw only rarely and never could remember—filled me with a sense of foreboding, of danger, of drugs and drunkenness. I was always glad to be out of there and on my way home.

Sonny, however, ate it up. He loved my dad no matter what the circumstance. He was the apple of my father's eye, his firstborn son. Sonny knew my dad much longer than I ever did. My dad and mom split up after Sonny was four years old, just before I was born, and by all accounts my dad was a good father to him in those first few years.

Alex, too, our half-brother, knew my dad better than I ever did, because Dad lived with Alex's mother for years after Alex was born. So Sonny and Alex always enjoyed these visits to Grandma's house that repulsed me. I was always the odd kid out. Needing much more from my father because I never knew him, while Sonny and Alex had a closer relationship to him owing to the accident of time and circumstance that defined my father's life. With Sonny, for his first four years; with Alex, for his first six years; with me, basically nothing.

In this situation vis-à-vis my relationship to my father—I have to say, as I look back on it now, that here, too, was the hand of my guardian angel, watching over me, protecting me and keeping me out of harm's way. Sonny and Alex both adored my father; they both had ample opportunity to bond with him as children; and my father never gave me the chance to know him. Sonny and Alex both followed in my father's footsteps; he was their role model.

My dad was a heroin addict for much of his adult life, during the formative years in the lives of Sonny and Alex. Sonny and Alex both developed an addiction to heroin, like my father. Alex told me once that our dad gave him his first heroin fix when Alex was still a teenager. Sonny and Alex both died of heroin overdoses, Alex at twenty-one years old, Sonny at thirty-eight. I have often wondered if that would have been my fate as well, had I chosen to follow in my father's footsteps, had I looked up to him, as Sonny and Alex both did.

My father knew I was not like Sonny and Alex. He could tell I resisted his allure. He could see that I looked at him with mistrust. He held this against me. I was the outlier, and he knew I could see through his sickness.

One time, at one of his parties when I was in my teens and trying to be civil with him, trying to be an adult, I asked him about the Navajo side of our family. I was trying to establish some kind of connection with him in this way. He told me that I have an Indian name. I said: "Oh really? That's cool. I didn't know that. What is it?" I asked.

The room got quiet. All eyes were on us, one to the other. My dad looked at me. A malicious grin began to break slowly on his face: "Your Indian name is Chief Cold Blood." The room exploded in laughter. They hooted. They fell over. They pointed at me with derision. Someone said to my father: "Good one, Lionel." My face turned red hot. He couldn't stop laughing. He knew the knife had gone deep, but he didn't care. He didn't realize at the time just how deep his knife had sunk.

That blow was fatal. I never recovered from it. I never tried to nor cared to see him again. I doubt it mattered to him.

Three sons, each with the same father, each growing up in similar circumstances, each with the same set of obstacles or barriers or risk factors in their lives. Two of them dead far too young. One of them, choosing a different path, the only one alive now to tell the story.

My father is no longer alive, either, and he came to a bizarre end that sounds too crazy to be true. All his life, my father lived with four addictions, by my count. He was addicted to women. He had more wives than I can remember counting. On his annual or semiannual excursions with Sonny and me throughout our childhood and early teen years, my father always had a new wife and another child or newborn on the way. I have lost track of all the half-brothers and -sisters I have. I only know that the world is populated with lots of Moisas of his doing.

His second addiction was booze. He liked to drink to get drunk; he liked to party and was always the life of the party, charming, gregarious, funny, flirty with the ladies, and he played the guitar, always good for a drink or two.

As I noted, my father liked the horses, and his requisite first stop after picking us up from home was to see his bookie at his favorite hangout in East Los Angeles—the Silver Dollar Bar on Whittier Boulevard, a mile or two from our home in the barrio. And, of course, he couldn't see his bookie and not drink.

And the most deleterious addiction my father had was to heroin. Any one of his habits could have been deadly for him—for example, an angry drunk man sticking my father with a knife for sleeping with his wife or flirting too much, say; or my dad ruining his liver drinking himself to death or in a drunk driving accident; or even getting in a fight with his bookie over a misplaced bet or some other argument in his illegal gambling endeavors. I always thought, for sure, that my father would overdose on heroin, like my brothers had done many years prior.

But my dad seemed to be bulletproof. I give him due credit for this, because he did somehow manage to break the cycle of all his addictions as he got older. In his midlife, he settled down with a woman who would brook no disrespect. Norma was tough as nails with some kind of power over him, and, yes, he was much older now and no longer had the appetite, I suppose, for running around as he did in his younger days.

Dad cut way back on his drinking, limiting himself to an occasional cold beer on a hot Los Angeles summer day, on the weekends. Maybe his doctor gave him an ultimatum, or, more likely, he realized he was slowly killing himself on booze and getting less enjoyment out of each hangover. My father was not a stupid man. Weak and flawed, yes, but he could read the writing on the wall when it suited him.

And he did get off the horse and stop shooting up after Sonny died, following by many years the death of Alex. When Sonny overdosed, my dad took Sonny's death hard, and it must have scared him sober. So he dodged all the bullets after living pretty much as recklessly as he wanted for most of his life, so his guardian angel must have had some powerful mojo, too, and he listened to her (or him).

Now, herein lies the irony surrounding the facts of my father's death, which, to me, is the perfect metaphor for that old grim reaper that sneaks up on you from behind. My father and his final wife, Norma, the one who would brook no infidelity, retired and moved from Los Angeles to the town of Mesquite, Nevada, not far from Las Vegas. The climate was warm and sunny and dry, perfect for older folks. Housing was affordable there, back then. And, being in Nevada, the town had its share of gambling casinos, which he and Norma liked to do a couple of times a month, just for fun, no real addictive issues at this point, anymore.

One Sunday afternoon, Norma and Dad drove out to their favorite casino for the Sunday dinner buffet—an inexpensive dining experience, and they would take a drink after dinner and go over to the casino side and play with their spare cash. Dad liked the roulette wheel, and Norma was into the nickel slots.

I can imagine her sitting at the slots and feeding the monster, her light brown wig a bit disheveled from all the activity, chain-smoking her Chesterfields, and every now and then the bells and lights on the slot would clang and a bunch of nickels would pour out all over the damp and stained casino carpet at her feet.

But on this fateful day, back at the restaurant, my dad was making his way through the salad bar buffet, scooping up his greens and pepperoncini, the garbanzo beans and red onions and cheddar cheese, all topped with a hefty portion of Thousand Island dressing. He shuffled along toward the end of the salad bar and then his foot stepped on a cherry tomato lying on the floor at his feet. His body went flying up and back, the salad and food tray going in all directions, and he landed square on his rear end on the hard linoleum floor, right in front of the sunflower seeds and croutons under the glass canopy.

My father had busted his hip and was rushed to the hospital straightaway, Norma crying and screaming at the casino staff and the ambulance drivers as she held my dad's hand on the twenty-minute drive to the hospital. My dad lay in the hospital for a few days recuperating, and here is the coup de grâce and the bizarre finale to this story.

While in the hospital, my dad contracted sepsis, apparently a rather common affliction of those who are hospitalized—a place where free-floating germs abound. He never made it out alive from the unit where he was recuperating with the cast on his hip.

Dad had beat the devil all his life, tempting fate at every turn and barely escaping all types of risky behavior in his youth. But once he turned his back on fate and embarked on a cleaner, safer lifestyle, the old grim reaper wagged his finger at Dad and told him: "And now I come for you, when you least expect it; when you thought you had passed Go and collected your two hundred dollars."

I had to ask my cousin more than once to tell me again how my father died. It seemed like such a cosmic joke, a comeuppance for all time. I've always maintained the firm understanding that anything can happen to anyone at any time. But this was a sad end to a crazy life that reminds me that we are not safe anywhere. Even at the salad bar.

I can add to this story only that my father did live the life that gave him the most fun, life to the fullest, and at least he died in the arms of the woman he came to love fully, faithfully, and happily ever after.

I have seen an old photograph of my father, Sonny, Jo Ann, and me, on one of those rare occasions when Dad came for us, standing together on the hot sidewalk in front of our place in the projects, my dad holding the hands of Sonny and me. It looks like it may have been Easter Sunday, because we are all dressed in our Easter Sunday finest—all hand-me-downs from our better-off cousins. I must have been six years old, Sonny, maybe ten. I am smiling like a fool, Sonny looks angry and aloof (perhaps he knew my dad was already drunk), and Jo Ann is standing off to the side, barely in the frame, a position that betrays her place as the outcast in this "family portrait." Jo Ann was not my father's child. My mother took the photo with her Kodak Brownie camera, a model popular in the 1950s.

This was not a very good photo. No one other than I looks happy at all. My father looks bored and anxious, his face resolute and grim with clenched teeth. No doubt he wants to get out of there and to the party at his mother's or his sister's house. Maybe the guy with the heroin is already at the party, and Dad wants to make sure he gets his share. The rest of my dad in the photo is equally revealing. He seems stiff in his ill-fitting suit, unnatural, lacking warmth, and without any connection to his two firstborn sons. "Get me out of here," I can almost hear him now, silently screaming out at the camera lens more than sixty-five years later.

My father used to like to say there was a curse on the Moisas. I heard him say it often. It was his excuse for the life he had chosen, for not winning at the track, for not holding down a job, for never catching a break, for being "saddled" with kids at too young an age, for the fate that befell his two favorite sons. I avoided my brothers' fate; less so because I was a different person, I will always believe, but rather because I have been blessed with a guardian angel who would whisper in my ear the words: *I will watch over you always*—words I took to heart, words I always believed, words that never failed me.

Sonny and Me

THE HOUSING PROJECTS WERE, indeed, a place where dreams die young, and I saw this with my own eyes, in my own family. I was in third grade. I was eight years old. My brother, Sonny, was twelve years old and in seventh grade. We went to the same grammar school, Resurrection. We would see each other in the hallways or in the schoolyard at lunchtime.

At this point in time, Sonny would not let me walk to school with him. I was a little kid; he wanted to walk with his friends instead. Mom sent us off to school at the same time each morning so that he could watch over me, but early on he made it clear to me that I was to keep a whole block behind him. Typical older brother attitude, of course.

One day when school ended for the day and all us kids were pouring out of our classrooms, I saw Sonny down the hallway walking with his friend, Desi. I ran up to them and said to Sonny: "Can I walk home with you guys?" I remember this day very well. I remember a definite sense of wanting to "bond" with Sonny and his pal, although this specific concept certainly would not have been in my internal or external vocabulary.

Sonny quickly turned on his heels to me and with a ferocity I had never experienced before from him, he grabbed me by my shirt and threw me up against the grey cinder block wall of the hallway. "No, you can't," he told me, his face right up against mine. "I don't want you to hang around with me; and if I ever catch you with any of my friends, I'll kick your ass. It's too late for me now, but you still have a chance."

Sonny let me go and pushed me away, and just as quickly turned back to his pal, and they walked away and down the stairs.

I was numb and dazed. I didn't know what to think or do. Tears welled up in my eyes, and the other kids walking and running nearby moved around me and onward like a river, closing up the space that Sonny and Desi had just occupied, the afternoon sunlight streaming in on the long, narrow hallway of Resurrection School.

By this point in Sonny's life, he had become a "bad boy." He had started hanging out with the kids who wanted to be gang members, though they were still a bit too young. He was bringing home bad report cards, with bad marks for behavior, comportment, and attendance, as well as for the academic subjects. He was disruptive in the classroom. My mom and new stepfather were being called in to the principal's office on a regular basis, and the arguments with Sonny behind closed doors in their bedroom were becoming a regular event at home at night.

Sonny was beginning to dress like a gang member after school and on weekends. Khaki pants, white "wifebeater" T-shirt, thick Dixie Peach pomade coating his hair, a defiant flattop haircut with "fenders" that all the gang members wore.

He would disappear from sight at the beginning of Saturday morning and not be seen until late into the evening, then come into the house without a word, sullen and sulking, and silently devour the dinner that Mom had set aside for him while my stepdad stood over Sonny at the kitchen table lecturing him on his behavior.

That fall day in the school hallway, when Sonny vehemently told me it was "too late" for him, I could not immediately fathom what he meant by that, but over time the picture became much clearer, even to a little eight-year-old boy. I was becoming ever more conscious of the widening gulf separating Sonny and me, not just in terms of our age and development but also in our dispositions. He was a young teenager, and I was still just a boy.

I also was seeing around me in the projects that gang warfare was near and real. I saw many gang fights on the large, open grassy spaces among the units we lived in. A dozen or more kids with chains, knives, or broken bottles kicking and fighting it out in bloody hand-to-hand combat, pouring across the area in waves, surging back and forth like a tide, then crashing together headlong in a wild melee of screams and curses, the residents locking their doors, peering out furtively from behind drawn curtains.

The constant presence of cops patrolling in cars and on foot, their hands on their billy clubs at the ready, acted like a powerful wedge among us kids, dividing us into those who were intimidated and fearful of running afoul of the law, and those who became defiant and resisted. I had seen with my own eyes the cops putting choke holds on kids Sonny's age, pushing them up against the walls of the projects or throwing them facedown on the sidewalk, knees in their backs.

The cops, of course, were all white and always itching for a fight. They looked even at us "good kids" with suspicion and malice. We were all the enemy.

I'll never forget Christmas Day when Sonny was twelve years old, this must have been 1960 or so. Sonny wanted a beige trench coat for Christmas, the kind all his friends were wearing. I remember the loud fights my mom and stepdad were having over this coat, because my stepdad was insisting they couldn't afford it and Sonny didn't deserve it. It cost twenty dollars at the time.

This number is permanently etched in my memory because of all the arguments between my mom and stepdad. I recall that this was about one-fourth the monthly rent we were paying at that time.

My mom had recently married Raul, mainly because he had a regular job and was a "good Catholic parishioner" (but more on that later); and as a result of her so-called "upward move" (also more on that later), we no longer qualified to live in the rent-controlled Estrada Courts reserved for those on welfare. At this point in my life, I was becoming aware of the cost of things, mostly from listening in on the constant fights over money that raged in the house, and I had, in my own way, begun to assimilate the crushing stresses of want and lack and to sense a burning need to escape the suffocating poverty that always hung over my family.

For despite Raul's steady income at a regular job with the phone company, Raul was still just another Mexican American in 1960s America, and we were still at the bottom of the income scale and still living in the barrio. Mom's marriage to Raul was less an upward move than a lateral shift and, in fact, became a real spiral downward for all the trouble he ended up causing us, emotionally, psychically, and traumatically. Our standard of living did not improve after she married him. In fact, our quality of life deteriorated significantly.

Their marriage eventually failed, to no one's surprise, based as it was on my mother's heartfelt but misguided attempt to escape the projects by marrying her way out of them. In fact, if she was trying to move us out of the projects and the gang dangers lurking there, she didn't do us any better. The houses we occupied after Raul was in our lives were never more than a few blocks from Estrada Courts, and the gang influence was always right around the corner. Mom never really loved Raul, she declared later. I feel bad for her, always making one bad choice after another.

So that fateful Christmas morning in 1960, when Sonny had been pleading with Mom for weeks for the trench coat he wanted, marked a watershed moment of dysfunction in our family. A sort of Waterloo dynamic, when the old, fragile order was now definitively collapsed, and a new, uncomfortable, and uneasy disquiet suffused every aspect of our lives together.

Our custom at Christmas in those days was for each of us to open one big gift in the evening after Christmas Eve dinner, usually a turkey with all the trimmings. When Sonny opened his gift-wrapped box and pulled out the trench coat, it was the happiest I had seen him in a long time. He went over to Mom and gave her a big kiss, and she was beaming. Raul just kind of half-smiled, it was more like a painful grimace. He was, no doubt, thinking of all the weekly payments he would have to be making for the next twelve months at Sears Roebuck. Sonny begged Mom to let him go out with his friends to show off his new trench coat, and she, filled with joy and Christmas spirit, told him, "Sure, go ahead, just come home by ten. Mass is at six, and you can wear your new coat to church."

The next morning, long before the first light of winter dawn appeared, full of excitement, I woke Jo Ann and said to her: "It's Christmas Day, Jo Ann! Let's go see what Santa Claus brought us." Sonny and I slept in the same bedroom, in bunkbeds, me on top and Sonny on the bottom, and he was not in his bed, even though he always slept late.

Jo Ann and I came into the living room, and Sonny, Mom, and Raul were in there, silent and grim. Sonny was sitting on the couch, stone-faced, Mom at the other end, red-eyed and chain-smoking her Lucky Strikes with an ashtray full of cigarette butts on her lap. Raul was pacing the room, clenching his fists, the anger etched deep and hard on his dark face. The tension in the room was suffocating.

Jo Ann and I had no idea what to do. I asked Mom if we could open our presents now, and Raul made some kind of dismissive comment that I could not make out. Mom said nothing. Sonny got up from the couch and went into the bedroom and slammed the door behind him.

Then I noticed the trench coat thrown haphazardly across a chair in the living room. It looked wrinkled, disheveled, discarded. As I walked over to the Christmas tree, I saw it—a large burn on the lapel, a cigarette burn, and a big wet stain, not quite dry yet, right across the front.

I don't remember anymore how the rest of our Christmas morning went, except that we did have to get ready right away for morning Mass, and only Mom and Jo Ann and I went this time, all of us walking quietly in the cold darkness, our feet on the sidewalk the only sound for that long and distraught twenty-minute walk to Resurrection Church. I remember Mom crying now and then throughout the Mass. The rest is a blur.

Later in the day, Mom told us what had happened. Sonny had come home drunk, and his brand-new trench coat was ruined with a cigarette burn near the lapel, and some kind of liquor stain on the front. He had gone out drinking with his friend Desi and the other "bad boys" that were an ever-present force in his life these days. There was little more that Mom and Raul could drag out of Sonny.

The day marked a real decisive and divisive moment in our household. The lines were now drawn, firm and clear, separating Sonny not only from Mom and Raul but also from me and Jo Ann. We were still innocents in many ways, and Sonny was now firmly set apart in his world of rebellion and animosity toward all authority, at home, at school, and in the world.

Sonny was never forced to come to Mass with us anymore. The moment delineated the hard-and-fast beginning of a never-ending series of fierce arguments and actual fistfights between Sonny and Raul, and constant bickering between Mom and Raul, mostly about Sonny but eventually about everything in our lives.

Sonny never wore his trench coat after that fateful Christmas Eve. One day, not long after, I was throwing out the household garbage and I saw the ill-starred coat in the trashcan. I wondered for a moment who had thrown it out. Was it Mom, so as not to ever be reminded of that awful moment when Sonny transformed before her eyes from a troubled boy to a hard and angry young man, now lost to her forever? Or perhaps it was Raul, in a fit of unholy rage as was his habit in those days. I looked around the yard at the glowing dusk of winter evening and at the pools of yellowed light cast by our windows on the scruffy turf that we called home.

I never learned the answer to this question, and when I closed the lid on the garbage that I had heaped on Sonny's misbegotten coat, I felt a cold wind in my face, and I shivered in the knowledge of being stuck in a place that no longer felt safe for any of us.

That warm, bright autumn day in the hallway at Resurrection School before that fateful Christmas was a confusing episode for me at the time. But it became clearer very soon in the days and weeks leading up to "the trench coat Christmas" episode, that Sonny was striding boldly and defiantly and with open arms toward the gang life that surrounded us and permeated our lives like the sickening, suffocating, toxic smog that filled our hot, hazy, thick brown days in the fifties and sixties in East Los Angeles.

Sonny joined a gang shortly thereafter, a fact confirmed by the blue gang tattoo he had etched into his skin in that space between his left thumb and index finger, the letters *VNE*, which stood for *Varrio Nuevo Estrada*—the gang that ruled our Estrada Courts neighborhood. On his inside right forearm another tattoo said *Con Safos*, a common emblem of gang life.

The rival gang he was expected to go up against was White Fence from the neighboring projects. But the real opposition force he would now do battle with for the rest of his life was the Los Angeles Police Department.

By the time Sonny was sixteen, he was serving a long sentence in the San Dimas juvenile detention center, in the desert, a two-hour drive from our barrio in East Los Angeles. He did time in county jail when he got older, and he developed a fondness for heroin, in addition to pot, pills of all kinds, and booze.

I have never stopped wondering, ever since that day in the school hallway, how Sonny could tell me or, more to the point, tell himself, that it was "too late" for him and that I still had a chance. He was protecting me from the life that he saw he was heading into. He was being my older brother in trying, in his own way, to shield me from the type of friends he had been hanging out with and that he knew would be a bad influence on me. He could see, apparently, that I was different from him, and not cut out for a gang life. He threatened to "kick my ass" if he saw me following his path.

My guardian angel has taken many shapes and forms over my long life, always protecting me or pulling or pushing me this way or that, toward safety, toward a better situation, out of harm's way. In that particular instance, my guardian angel took the shape of Sonny, a real person, a genuine living being, a force telling me in no uncertain terms to stay away from the life that he had chosen for himself and threatening real consequences if I did.

I have no doubt that Sonny would have made good on his promise to hurt me if he saw me moving closer to him, following him on his destructive path, and I thank him and love him for the care he showed me, in his own way, that day after school.

We didn't have much in common from that point onward. I took his advice. I did what I could to steer clear of him and his friends. I am sorry for not having a brother that I could relate to, hang out with, have a normal brother relationship with. I could have loved my big brother, as I have loved my little sister.

I have proven to myself that I can be a good brother to other men I have become close to over the years, my brothers from another mother and father, and I am sorry that it could not be Sonny.

But I am more sorry for that little boy in Sonny, the boy who, at such an early age, felt that it was too late for him, saw that his destiny was filled with danger, limited options, trouble with the cops and with society.

My brother Sonny was not a gangbanger. He was not a criminal. He was not a bad guy. Sonny was kind and funny, and endeared himself to everyone he met. He was like a gentle giant. He never killed anyone nor got in trouble for any kind of violent crime.

He got busted for possession of pot, small amounts, as I recall, and more often than not, his only crime was being in the wrong place at the wrong time, and for being Mexican American at a time when the cops and the whole system was geared to throwing kids like him in jail at the slightest wayward turn.

Sonny made the kind of bonehead mistakes that got him in trouble not because he was bent on fighting the system but because the system was bent on fighting him, criminalizing him, and trying to beat some common sense into him—beginning with my stepfather, with the teachers, then the cops and the criminal justice system. Sonny was hurt more than angry. Sonny was let down far more often than he was lifted up. Sonny was a victim of too many people ready to take him down for the crime of being a wounded, struggling kid who had no one who cared for him in the best way.

I know why Sonny joined a gang at a young age. It's as plain as day, and all the social psychologists and juvenile behaviorists know this as gospel truth today. Sonny wanted to be accepted. He wanted to belong. He wanted to feel connected to someone. And he never got that at home. Sonny was just like me, actually. We just found our acceptance in different places.

I know his pain. I felt the same forces arrayed against me that he did, beginning with my mother, then with my father, then with my stepfather. The only difference between us was that my guardian angel showed me how to avoid the edge of the cliff, how to walk back from danger. I don't know why Sonny's guardian angel couldn't do the same for him. What part fate? What part luck? What part destiny?

How does a child at that young age see his world in such stark terms, closed off from the good? How is it that he resigned himself at such an early age to such a destructive life? Sonny eventually died of a heroin overdose when he was thirty-eight, lying on a dirty bathroom floor, blue in the face, with a needle stuck in his vein.

On the night before we buried my brother, I had an awful dream that the fates had it in for the Moisa brothers. I was afraid that I, too, would die young from some fatal flaw inherent in our genes. I woke up shaking and drenched in sweat, and I saw Sonny standing there beside my bed, as real and as sure as I have ever seen him in life. He looked at me and smiled, and he said to me: "Don't worry, little brother, you're gonna live to be a very old and happy man."

Then he disappeared. I will never forget that dream/not dream. I will always be grateful that Sonny cared enough for me to push me away from the path that he felt was his to walk, the cross he felt was his, and his alone, to bear.

Sonny and I didn't share much of a life together. Our actual brotherhood was short lived, indeed, but I will always hold him close in my heart. Even though he and I were very different people and ended up following different paths, we both suffered from the same affliction, we both shared a common blood that poured from a common wound that never healed. We both know the trouble we've seen. *Sometimes I feel like a motherless child.*

Sonny left behind a son or two or three. We all lost count of the women in his life. He would disappear for long stretches of time, then come by unannounced to Mom's house or to Jo Ann's, high as a kite, his eyes glistening with the drug, his movements slow and easy, his voice smooth and mellow. He named all his sons Eddie, his own name, so that he would never forget their names, he once told me. I thought he was joking, but I was wrong, and I see, now, it does make some kind of sense if you are not in your children's lives long enough to recognize their faces.

His eldest son, Eddie Number One, was twelve years old when Sonny died, and he came to the funeral and to the burial later at the cemetery. We have photos, and Eddie seemed happy on that day and, in a way, liberated of the burden of never having to wonder when he would see his father again. I know he was happy to be with family, my father, his grandfather, whom he never knew.

Eddie told me later that day when we were alone that he once saw my father come out of a bar in the old neighborhood. When Eddie recognized him and called his name, my father pretended he didn't see or hear him, but he did, and he turned quickly, awkwardly, back into the bar to avoid any confrontation or even the slightest conversation with his first grandson. I know Eddie was still hurt at this slight. I had felt this same sting from my father's insults to me. I could see the discomfort in my father trying to be with us at the funeral, again, that old dynamic of wishing he were anywhere else but here, hoping no one would bring up anything too uncomfortable for him to deal with.

But then, isn't that what families do at weddings and funerals? They put aside everything else, no matter how awkward, in the name of some abstract, undefined, and often absurd concept of family?

As Eddie got older, into his teen years, Jo Ann and her husband, Mike, being generous souls and all about family, offered to take Eddie in to live with them in Eureka, away from the old neighborhood and its negative influences and painful memories. They wanted to give him a new start in life. A stable home, some new environment to offset the difficult life he had behind him.

Although I never knew this to be true, and cannot personally attest to it, the rumor in the family at the time was that Eddie's mother also was a junkie, like Sonny, and Eddie had seen too much of too many bad things for Jo Ann and Mike to bear. So Jo Ann and Mike drove down to Los Angeles, packed Eddie's meager belongings in their pickup and took him into their home. They have always been so good like that. Wonderful parents, loving family, staying in touch always with everyone. Ready to visit kin anywhere at the drop of a hat. I admire them for that.

And here, now, is the part that is so difficult to tell. Eddie started out happy and well adjusted, like a brother to his two cousins, Jo Ann and Mike's young son and daughter. This seemed like it was going to be the story with a happy ending, Jo Ann caring for her older brother's son that he cared so little for.

But Eddie was haunted by demons too powerful to exorcise. After finishing high school here in Eureka in my sister's home, Eddie began to move in the wrong circles. He stayed out late, seemed to fall in with a bad crowd, met a young woman, and eventually sired a boy out of wedlock. He began to have a bad reputation in this small town. One of Mike's good friends had given Eddie a good job, as a favor to Mike, and the friend eventually told Mike that Eddie was not quite working out so well.

Eddie borrowed a substantial amount of money from his boss, Mike's friend. He also borrowed a lot of money from me. To me, he gave a real touching sob story about his son and needing lots of money to fix his car so he could see his son. But he never did see his son, his common-law wife told us. Then one day soon thereafter, Eddie disappeared, taking with him some of the more expensive power tools that belonged to his boss.

This was a bridge too far. He had turned his back on the unconditional love and affection and caring that Mike and Jo Ann had shown him. He had borrowed a bundle from me that he obviously had no intention of paying back. But we were family. This can happen in family sometimes. I get that. But Eddie had betrayed the trust of someone outside the family, someone who had helped him as a favor to Mike by giving Eddie a good job.

Eddie disappeared for a long time after that. Jo Ann and Mike were heartbroken. A number of unusual reincarnations of his life brought him in and out of our lives for a few years, but never long enough or consistently enough to see any maturity on his part. In fact, he always seemed to be working some con on us, though we never were tempted to lend him any more money. I am compressing time and conflating a lot of events to make this narrative make sense.

But the essential facts are that Eddie now appeared to be a homeless drug addict, following his father's path in this strange journey of life. I know he was aware of where it would lead. I know he got a decent break in his young and difficult life from Jo Ann and Mike who truly loved and cared for him.

Eddie was living on the banks of the dry bed of the Los Angeles River, in a homeless encampment with a few other crazy characters. He obviously had enough money to buy a smartphone and to post some of the strangest videos and photos I ever care to see.

We have seen these selfie videos, because after the inception of Facebook, Jo Ann found Eddie's Facebook page as she was doing a search, hoping against hope to find him. I wish she had not found him there, because Eddie's behavior had become even more bizarre, and he was not shy about exposing this.

It seemed to us that Eddie's brain was fried on some undetermined drug(s). He seemed too far gone for normal homeless behavior even. And stranger still, Eddie had adopted a Lucifer-like persona. A name that is too crazy to even comprehend, Lucius Rothschild. Sometimes he would change his Facebook page to show he was now Eddie Charles Lucifer Rothschild.

Later, he became Dr. Edward Charles Lucifer Rothschild, PhD, founder and CEO of Tech Alchemy. Doctor Rothschild? Really? Eddie never went to college. As I recall, he was lucky to graduate high school.

The self-loathing I had understood to be at the core of my father's addictions and my mother's addiction to religion (the opiate of the people) was now evident in Eddie as he assumed an alternate persona, a whole different name, the ultimate escape from self. Interesting that he "founded" a company with the name of alchemy. Alchemy is the magical process of converting base metals into gold. It seems Eddie had gone in the opposite direction and converted his gold into a base metal.

Not only did Eddie adopt a different name in his drug-induced incarnations, he once posted on his Facebook page an explanation about his *other* last name, Moisa, his rightful name that continued to appear on Facebook now and then. Following are his words, taken from his Facebook page in early 2020:

"OK, everyone it's been asked quite a bit. What's with the last name Moisa that you appear to go by besides rothschild. Good question! Easy answer! Moisa is the name of a society based out of Rome, Italy, 'The MOISA Society' so it's not my last name per say it's just a society that was named after me. . . . Everyone who joins and is apart of the MOISA Society is a 'moisa' or apart of the moisa society. By the way Lionel just happens to be the first name of Lionel Rothschild my grandfather."

His real last name is Moisa, we all know that and it's on his birth certificate, so he was in serious denial and created a crazy untenable explanation for it. And his grandfather's first name was Lionel, yes, but his last name is our last name, Moisa.

This is self-loathing of the highest order, or lowest order, I should say. Gold to base metal. Why Eddie would choose this downwardly-spiraling path when he had a clear alternative with Jo Ann and Mike is beyond me, a genuine outpouring of love and caring. But then, I am sure he saw stuff when he was a child living with a junkie mother that I can only imagine. I feel bad for him. And yes, we truly are all on our own path, and there is nothing anyone can do for us as we follow our own destiny, guided by our own star, wherever it leads us.

My father's "curse of the Moisas" seems to carry over from one generation to the next, ad nauseam. It is intergenerational trauma of the highest order. I wonder when this curse will be broken. How long before the spell is lifted. I know there are many other "little Eddies" out there,

Sonny's progeny. I wonder what they know of their father and how they have lived out their lives.

Do they suffer under this curse and have no idea why their lives are so messed up? Or have they made the leap past the bad karma and found a path that makes better sense for them than it did for my father, and for Sonny, and for his son, the first Eddie?

I wonder where Eddie's guardian angel is. Sleeping on the job? Not there at all? Or biding her time, waiting for the right moment, in a vast concept of cosmic time that we mere mortals are not privy to. The moment may be waiting still, when Eddie is in a position to hear his own guardian angel's words—the words I have always taken to heart, the words I have always believed in, the words that never seemed to fail me.

I can only pray that for Eddie it is not too late. He is no longer posting anything on Facebook. Perhaps his body was found by some stranger on a dirty bathroom floor in a city park, a needle stuck in his vein.

Not a day goes by that I don't think about Sonny. There are mornings still that I wake up crying from some awful dream about him. I am sure he is looking down on me all the time, being my big brother in my dream the day we buried him, or as he was on that autumn day at Resurrection School, protecting me from harm, and telling me: *I will watch over you always.* I am sure he is watching over his son, the first Eddie, and all the other little Eddies he has left behind.

Ernie

J O ANN IS MY half-sister, though we are as close and connected to each other as two full siblings can ever be. Jo Ann and I have always played together from our earliest days, and we have stayed close ever since. Jo Ann's father is Ernie, the one and only true love of my mother's life. The story of this relationship reads like a modern-day Romeo and Juliet, with different circumstances, for sure, but with the same tragic, star-crossed consequences.

My mother and Ernie were sweethearts at Lincoln High School in East Los Angeles during World War II. The pair were "Hollywood beautiful." He looked like a teenage Errol Flynn or a Mexican James Dean, with soulful eyes, a thick lower lip, a face like Adonis, and curly-loose black hair.

Mom's pictures from that time reveal a young version of Rosalind Russell. Mom has never told us many stories about that time, but the basic outlines have become clear and the stuff of family legend.

Ernie was a year older than my mom, and when he graduated, he turned his back on my mom and married another girl. The reasons have never been known to us kids. In my attempt once to create a novel of this story, I fantasized that Ernie had been betrothed to this girl at birth, in some old Mexican tradition uniting two aristocratic families, forced to marry a woman he did not love and hardly knew. But this was my writer's romantic embellishment of a story that has enough tragedy in it as it stands. The truth is even more heartbreaking than any fantasy I could possibly create.

Ernie's marriage, of course, broke my mother's heart. She dropped out of high school in her senior year and took off with a girlfriend by train to Tennessee, where her friend had some family. As it turns out, my mom lived with her friend's family in Oak Ridge, the site of the Manhattan Project, one of two sites where they created the atomic bomb. This has nothing to do with anything, other than an interesting little factoid.

After a short stay in Tennessee, Mom returned to Los Angeles, and this is when she married my father. The three of them, my father, my mother, and Ernie, were all good friends at Lincoln High. They hung out together all the time. My mom, it seems, married my dad on the rebound, a fact that he never tired of telling us, as if he had never let go of the pain of being her second choice, the man she had to settle for, when her one true love left her so suddenly.

But Ernie never left my mother's heart. And this is what my father could never forget nor forgive. At some point, Ernie and Mom became lovers again. I don't know who strayed first, my dad with the mother of Alex, my half-brother, or Mom with Ernie, but this is how it all came down. What follows is a tragic chronology of pain and misbegotten lives, modern love and classic drama.

Here is how it all plays out. My older brother, Sonny, is born, and my dad and mom are living happily ever after in a nice little house in El Monte. Four years later, I am conceived, followed five months later by Alex, conceived by my dad's girlfriend. My dad and mom split up, and my dad disappears from my life. I am born, I go into the foundling hospital at birth; six months later Mom changes her mind, finds me, and takes me home; four months after I am home, Mom conceives Jo Ann, Ernie's daughter.

Sonny is four years older than I, Alex on the other side of town is five months younger than I, and Jo Ann, Ernie's daughter, is fourteen months younger than I. My mom has three kids from two fathers and is struggling with no means of support. It is the East Los Angeles barrio in the 1950s. Everything is a struggle for my mom. It gets worse.

Ernie doesn't disappear after Jo Ann is born. He continues to come around to the projects to see his daughter and my mom. I remember his visits clearly, through the smoggy haze of childhood memory. Ernie always brings us shiny red candy apples. I can still hear myself yelling through the screen in the living room window from outside as I see Ernie walking down the sidewalk to our place, 3362 Hunter Street. "Ernie's coming! He has candy apples!"

All of us kids squeal with delight. My mom has dressed up Jo Ann real nice, with her best Easter dress and freshly combed hair. Then, Ernie makes a big show of giving us two boys our candy apples, and Mom tells us to play outside while she, Jo Ann, and Ernie spend the time together in the house. I remember this happening often. The story gets worse.

Ernie had a congenital heart defect. My mom knew this at the time, she has told us later. Then, suddenly, Ernie stopped coming and he stopped calling. My mom never called his home, for all the obvious "other woman" reasons. Ernie by now had two kids with his wife, so it was the typical, all-too familiar story of infidelity and secret lovers. After some weeks, Mom is unable to contain her fears, and she finally relents and calls Ernie's brother, praying that he answers the phone.

Ernie had died in the operating room, Ernie's brother told Mom, while they were performing experimental open-heart surgery. Ernie never told my mom about this procedure he would have to undergo. But the night before he went into surgery, he told his brother, for the first time, about his love affair with my mom, and about his little four-year-old daughter, Jo Ann. Ernie's brother kept all this from his family, and let the story be buried in the grave with Ernie.

I cannot imagine the grief my poor mother carried. I have seen only the consequences of her pain. I have, however, heard my dad, ever selfish and self-serving, telling Sonny and me many years later, after we all knew the story, that he had known all along that Mom loved Ernie more than she loved my dad. This was his takeaway from the tragedy that afflicted our house.

In her adult years, Jo Ann tracked down her half-sister and half-brother, Ernie's kids with his wife, and Ernie's brother, still alive to tell the story that he had kept secret for over fifty years. Now everyone knows, and Jo Ann corresponds with her new family.

The congenital problem with Ernie was a hole in his heart. A hole in his heart. You couldn't write better fiction. I leave the truth unvarnished.

My mother seemed always to be terribly unlucky in love. She lost or, rather, never had the first and only man she ever loved. She married my father because she couldn't have Ernie, and that union turned out to be a mistake. Then she married Raul, and he turned out to be an even bigger mistake. She divorced Raul and eventually consigned herself to a convent in her fifties and decided she wanted to become a nun. Yes, a convent; yes, a nun; but even her "marriage to Christ" ended in failure.

I tell this story not as background to my own story but to my mom's. It helps explain some of the anguish, grief, and trauma she has endured in her long and difficult life. I cry for her sometimes when I think about all this, as I cry, still, for the little boy that she felt she could not hold onto, either as a newborn or as a seventeen-year-old kid experiencing love for the first time. But that is another story.

I know that my mom, too, has been abandoned by love, and I am sorry she never had her own guardian angel telling her those words that I have always been comforted by—*I will watch over you always.*

ERNIE

William Sharp wrote that the heart is a lonely hunter. With love comes pain, in the wanting, in the having, in the losing. Like death, no one can elude the sorrow that love brings. But death is an essential fact of life, and love is the only thing that makes life worthwhile. For at the end of our life, our worth is not measured by how much we had in possessions but by how much we gave in love. Lennon and McCartney said that love is all you need.

until

until you have known the blood-drenched horrors of war,
you cannot know the true meaning of peace.

until you have seen the charred and mangled limbs of children
lying in the smoldering streets,
the eyes of dead women and men gouged out,
their tongues, swollen and purple,
hanging out of hollowed heads,
bodies contorted in ghastly repose,
stiff and infested with maggots,
you will not know what it is to sleep easy

until you have stared, gape-mouthed in disgust,
the green vomit welling up from deep in your belly,
your head unable to turn aside,
your eyes unable to look away,
you shall not know true calm within your soul.

my heart has been a battlefield of dread,
sacked and plundered,
disemboweled and stuck on a pike,
left for dead by the wayside
and scavenged by foul carrion.

my love has had its tongue cut out and fed to the sharks
that swarm around me as my little boat, capsized,
sinks slowly to the deep.

my cries for mercy are mocked by my enemies,
they make joke of my pitiful state,
and laugh to hear me sob,
left alone and abandoned by my friends.

UNTIL

i do not know how long i can continue like this,
putting on a brave face,
marching onward to the next battlefield,
or retreating from another smoking stinking
landscape of bombshell craters and unrecognizable ruins
as the dead pile up around me,
their voices, now, as wind whistling through rotting bones.

i see all around me the destruction wrought by love betrayed.
i hear behind me the medics carrying away the faceless corpses of love lost.
i feel the abiding fear of foxhole loneliness that pierces my gut like a bayonet.

i trudge on, exhausted, to my uncertain fate,
my legs too weak to move,
my will too numb to resist.

i wonder now, too late, i'm sure,
if i should have long ago negotiated a truce with love,
laid down my weapons of pride, ego, absurd notions of dignity,
and sued for the peace that i had convinced myself was false.

i have fought too many battles for love that ended in a draw.
i have been too quick to declare victory
when my destiny determined, instead, ignominious defeat.

perhaps i should have surrendered long ago, i say to myself.
perhaps there is no price of peace too high to pay,
no ransom enough to redeem my respect.

i have known for too long the abominable horrors of war on this
surreal battlefield of the heart,
and i long for the peace that comes, not with death,
but at the hands of an ally who waits just beyond
the next scorched and desolate ridge,
a glass of cool water in her hand, a warm bed to lie in,
and a comforting word: *yes, the war is over;*
sleep now, in these arms that enfold you.

I'm Santa Claus

Raul was without a doubt the biggest mistake my mom made in her long and sad legacy of disastrous relationships. She married him for money, or at least for more money than a welfare check twice a month. When he realized that she had no love for him, things turned very bad or, rather, worse.

The problems didn't wait until he became aware that he had been duped into a loveless marriage. Raul came out slugging almost as soon as the wedding bells had finished their mournful ringing.

My mom and Raul got married in late September when I was in second grade. Three months later, we celebrated our first Christmas together with this stranger in our lives. Sonny was eleven years old, I was only seven, Jo Ann was five. Christmas was still a big thing for all of us. Jo Ann and I still believed, or we wanted to believe, in Santa Claus, in the way children hang onto that quality of charming innocence that is their right.

Our first Christmas morning with Raul began in the usual way that was our custom. Jo Ann and I woke up first. We always had a pact that we confirmed on Christmas Eve before going to sleep. "Promise me you'll wake me up as soon as you see that Santa Claus has come," we would tell each other. "Yes, I promise." Then, we would turn off the light and close our eyes, both of us doing our best to calm the mounting excitement in our little tummies.

I don't remember now who woke up first, but, once the initial scouting out had been completed and confirmed that Santa Claus had arrived, the other one was awakened with the exciting news: "Santa Claus came! Santa Claus came!" With squeals and shouts we woke up Sonny, ran downstairs, and jumped around the tree, examining the gifts, eyeing the big stocking below the tree filled with nuts of all kinds and fruits, and one of us would plug in the lights so that the living room was filled with Christmas cheer.

My mom and Raul came downstairs from the bedroom and the familiar annual ritual of joy began. Mom directed us which gifts we could open first, since we had morning Mass to attend at six a.m. and most of the gifts would be saved for after our return home. We took turns tearing open our gifts, squealing with delight, kissing Mom with thanks, and thanking Santa Claus wherever he was at that point in the world, finishing up his important work for all the little children this Christmas Day.

Then, it was time to get ready and attend church. When we returned from Mass, our breakfast that morning was not the usual oatmeal, but we could eat any of the fruits and nuts from our overstuffed red plastic mesh "stockings." We loved Christmas. For all her problems, money woes, and concerns, Mom always did make a great Christmas for us, no doubt about it.

Mom was upstairs, busy with something, I don't know what. The gifts were, by now, all scattered across the living room, under the tree, lying on the sofa, here and there some tattered remnants of gift wrap. Raul was sitting on the sofa, looking at everything, and Jo Ann came over to him with the gift that "Santa" had brought her—usually the one big-ticket item we had specifically requested in our letters to the North Pole that we had written earlier in the month. "Look what Santa brought me, Raul," she told him in all sweet innocence and naïve joy.

Raul looked at Jo Ann and without missing a beat said to her: "I'm Santa Claus." It was a terse, clenched-fist, cold-blooded statement. He dug in deeper as Jo Ann's little brow furrowed while she stared at him in complete lack of comprehension.

"There isn't any Santa Claus, don't you understand?" he said. "I'm the one who paid for all your toys." I was there in the living room and saw this too. I instantly understood that my seven-year-old suspicions were finally confirmed by a grown-up, although I did not expect to be so brutally and suddenly disabused of my childhood fantasies.

Jo Ann started to cry and ran from the room and up the stairs to her bedroom. I followed her up and closed the door behind us. We held each other close and cried together. It was the end of innocence, and it was hideous.

We told our mom later that day what had happened. She was shocked and speechless. She didn't know how to right the wrong, how to put the genie back in the bottle. The damage was done, she knew and we knew. We never heard the fight that must have ensued between the two of them.

Raul was an insecure man who did not know how to love or be generous in any way with himself or his stuff, not even to children. He just had to let us know that he was the one we should be thanking for what we got from him. He had no joy inside, and he could not abide seeing joy in anyone else. He could not let us have Christmas Day if it meant he had to stand aside and let Santa Claus take the credit for our happiness.

The man was small and stingy and hard inside in every way imaginable. I am sure he wanted us to fall down on our knees at every meal and give thanks to him. But, of course, he had to contain his resentment and jealousy of God as he led us in the standard prayer of grace before our meals: "We thank you, God, for these, thy gifts, which we are about to receive, from thy bounty through Christ, our Lord, amen." I have no doubt he would have preferred that we include his name alongside God's in our prayer of thanksgiving.

Jo Ann and I had matching stuffed bunny rabbits that we got one Easter Sunday. We had named them Easter and Esther. We'd had them for maybe three years—two cute, little boy-and-girl stuffed toys, one pink, one blue. All little children have something like this, a security blanket, a stuffed animal, something they love and cherish and hold on to every waking and sleeping minute. We played with them all the time; we bonded together with them. We made up our little fantasy life with them. We were never without them.

Raul hated that we loved these little bunnies. He told us we were too old to be playing with dolls. One day—this was just a few months after Raul and my mom married and shortly after that first awful "I'm Santa Claus" Christmas—I found our Easter and Esther in the trash. Raul had thrown them out.

I pulled our little stuffed bunnies from the trash, took them to Mom, and she did her best to clean off the coffee grounds and cigarette ash from their fuzzy little bodies. She was boiling mad underneath her skin, you could tell, and no doubt sickened to her stomach at what she had wrought upon her kids.

This is how things started out for us with Raul. From there, it only got worse. The next traumatic event I recall with sickening clarity was less than two years into the marriage, when my mom was pregnant with Carol, Raul's child. You would think that impending fatherhood would make the man more human, softer, more considerate of his legacy, or sensitive to the needs of children in general. But you would be wrong.

By now we were out of the projects, living just a few blocks away in a small, two-bed, one-bath house on Garnet Street. All us kids were crowded in one bedroom, Sonny and I in the bunkbeds, Jo Ann in her own bed. She was eight, I was not quite ten years old, and Sonny was almost fourteen. Mom was far enough along in her pregnancy that she was showing. Pregnancy was not a blessed event for Mom. She complained all the time.

I don't know how the fight started. I was in the kitchen alone. Everyone else was at home, it was late in the afternoon on a weekend day. I forget what I was doing but then I heard it, shouts from Raul and screaming from my mom and Jo Ann and Sonny. I threw open the kitchen door, and there I saw Mom sprawled on a chair in the living room, with Raul standing over her and strangling her with his bare hands.

Sonny had jumped on Raul's back and was pummeling his head and yelling at him to stop. Jo Ann was trying to pull his arms away from Mom and crying. Jo Ann later told me that she saw a pair of scissors on the table next to her and thought about grabbing them and sticking them in Raul's back, but there was too much going on for her to decide what she should do.

I stood there in the doorway between the kitchen and the living room, my feet frozen to the floor in fear, immobilized by the trauma, in the same way a person is unable to run from danger in a nightmare or tries to shout out but is unable to. I don't remember how long this violence lasted before Raul let go of Mom, she choking and crying and gasping for breath.

He left the house, still in a rage, and the rest of us were left crying and shocked and now afraid for our lives, doing our best to comfort Mom, a sense of anger and violence now rising up in each of us in our own way.

Things were never the same anymore for Mom and us kids after that. But for Raul, he seemed to go on with his life as if nothing had happened. We all went to church every Sunday, where he smiled and chatted with all the other parishioners, a "good Catholic man," everyone would say about him. Stella is a lucky woman to find a man like him, her with three kids and all.

Mom told us years later that she forced Raul to go with her to our local pastor, Father Garcia, for marriage counseling. But after hearing my mom tell her story, the priest just said that they needed to work things out. Apparently, attempted murder was not a matter of concern for Holy Mother Church in those days. I am sure Mom felt abandoned and ignored by the Roman Catholic Church that she loved so much. I wonder what our pastor would have said if Raul had succeeded in killing Mom. And this is the disgusting thing that I recall with such revulsion after that and after many more traumatic and violent episodes between Raul and Sonny.

Things got progressively worse between Raul and Sonny very quickly after Raul had tried to murder my mother. The two of them had a lot of fistfights, usually when Sonny was heading out the door to hang out with his friends and get away from the house. The trench coat episode was behind us, but the anger continued to boil, never far below the surface of their relationship. I recall on one occasion Raul tried to drag Sonny back in the house to prevent him from leaving—lifting him up and attempting to carry Sonny over his shoulder like an angry, struggling sack of potatoes.

And through it all, Raul continued to put on the face of a "good Catholic man," a "good parishioner," as men in those days were judged in our community of Resurrection Parish. He continued serving in the local chapter of the Knights of Columbus, bowing his head devoutly at Mass, and smiling at everyone who admired this good man for marrying a poor woman from the projects and saddled with three kids.

Raul was a pure hypocrite, and this was the first instance I ever knew of what this word means: someone evil when no one is looking, but all sweetness and light when he is out in public in front of other people. I used to get angry at everyone for thinking he was such a good man, a holy man. This was all that people cared about, that you appeared to be a "good Catholic." Hypocrisy became my beef with the Roman Catholic Church. The huge disconnect between professed values and the true state of a man's heart. This realization would eventually turn me away in disgust from the church.

Among the things Mom began to share with us kids as we got older—so much older so quickly in that awful house—was that Raul told her early on in their marriage that "she loved her kids more than she loved him." Insecure, jealous, small, stingy, and utterly unable to comprehend motherhood and what a mother feels for her kids.

Raul was also jealous of the dog that Mom had wanted as she got more advanced in her pregnancy. It was an adorable little cocker spaniel that Mom named Taffy, and we all loved that dog. Mom needed that dog to give her comfort, I later came to understand, as she realized what kind of man she had married.

I actually heard Raul tell her that she loved the dog more than she loved him. I suppose he was right, but that was on him. Sadly, Raul made Mom give up Taffy, I don't know how. But one day, suddenly, the dog was gone, and Mom was bereft for days. I remember Mom once confiding in us that there was something seriously wrong about a man who could not love animals.

We had a string of pets—dogs, cats—that all eventually suffered the same fate at Raul's hands. One day, suddenly, our beloved pet would disappear, and, cry as we might, no one would tell us where our pet was.

Mom did tell us when we were older that whenever Raul would announce to her that he had decided it was "time to get rid of that animal," that she begged him to take the poor animal out in the country and let it run free, hoping it would eventually find a good home. But she always suspected that he would never have bothered wasting the time and gas on that foolhardy, considerate gesture. No doubt, he just took the poor animal to the local pound to be put down.

Raul didn't want Mom to have a life that didn't include him. When John Kennedy was running for president, my mom got involved in his campaign as a volunteer with a group of Catholic women in the parish. The Democratic convention that nominated JFK was held in Los Angeles, and my mom's local group was part of a larger contingent that was invited to attend the big event.

Mom was so thrilled to be going; everyone was excited that a Catholic man might be president. And he was such a young and handsome man. On the day the group was to attend the convention, Raul called the local organizer and told her my mom was sick and couldn't go.

My mom sat in her best dress and her make-up, I can see her still, waiting and waiting on the sofa in vain all day for that carpool to come pick her up. She didn't find out until she called her friend the next morning. I don't know how that fight went, but it must have been nuclear.

When my dad learned that Mom had married Raul, that's when my dad started showing up more often than once or twice a year. The scenes were always the same. He would arrive, he would tell Mom to get us boys ready because he was going to take us for the day; then Raul would step into the picture, an argument would ensue because Raul insisted that my dad pony up money that Dad never provided for our child support, then the argument would escalate into an actual fistfight outside in the front yard.

That's when Dad would leave without us. I came to realize that my dad did not suddenly have a great epiphany of love and decided he wanted to be with his sons. He was merely "marking his territory" like a dog. Staking his claim in the presence of another dog near his litter.

Despite the strangulation incident and all the other tribulations and stresses that Raul put my mother (and us) through, I think the last straw for her was the one in which she saw her last hope of financial salvation squandered right before her eyes. Of course, it would come down to money for my mom.

Raul and his brother each owned a 50-percent interest in the home that Raul's parents occupied in Los Angeles, not far from us. Long before my mom married Raul, he and his brother had put up the down payment on this house and kept up the payments for his parents. Mom knew when she married Raul that he owned half of this important asset. Indeed, she believed this asset could be turned into equity for the house she hoped she and Raul would eventually buy for us.

Raul apparently did nothing to disabuse her of this misconception. For many years, every Sunday after Mass, we would pile into the car, an aging yellow Rambler that he had bought from his brother for too much money (my mom's words), and we would drive way out of the barrio of East Los Angeles, to the burgeoning suburbs of Anaheim, Santa Ana, West Covina, Tustin, and San Bernardino. We went there looking at all the booming housing developments springing up with their little flags flying around the newly built unfinished suburbs and walking through countless model homes that were selling for $30,000 plus.

Mom took a very active interest in finding the home that would take us out of the barrio, and every Sunday morning she would hand Raul a folded area of the real estate section of the *LA Times*. After Mass, we would pack a bag of lunch and drive the hour plus to search for our destiny. Raul obliged Mom with her little daydream.

But one day, all that lying ended, the charade undone. We never went out to see model homes again. Mom never looked at another real estate listing ever. She later told us what had changed. Without a word to my mom, Raul had long ago signed over to his brother his share of the equity in the home that he and his brother had held an equal interest in, so that his brother could take that equity and buy a home for himself and move out of the barrio. Raul's brother had done to us what Mom had been planning to do to him. Raul had sabotaged my mom's dream to help finance his brother's dream. There was no longer any "cookie jar" of equity that we could use to buy a home. Mom had been hoodwinked, and Raul had known all along that he would be doing this, and all those Sunday drives for hours and hours looking at fake homes had become a fake endeavor in itself. Raul had never intended for us to own a home. Instead, with one signature on a quit claim, Raul had given away his equity to his brother.

That was the real beginning of the end for Mom and her dreams of buying her way out of the barrio. Things settled into a moribund status quo for the rest of their married lives together. Mom had married Raul "for his money." In the end, he got the last laugh on that count, taking away from her clutches whatever money he had, stealing her dream, and impoverishing her life once again with another bad relationship. I pity my mom and Raul. She wanted his money, and he wanted her love. In the end, neither of them got what they came for.

This was the final blow. As my mom's marriage to Raul dragged on and on with no relief in sight, she became even more distant and found different ways to remove herself from the arena of conflict. But in so doing, she left us kids behind and helpless to fend for ourselves, to deal with Raul's hideous behavior in her absence. And she did all this with his blessings, because she occupied herself in "the work of the church." Makes me sick, still, to think about it.

Mom signed up to teach catechism to the Catholic kids in the local public grammar school, Lorena Street School. It was called "release time classes," and it was a formal arrangement between the public school system in Los Angeles and each local Catholic parish that allowed Catholic students to leave public school classes an hour early each weekday to attend catechism—Catholic religion classes.

So every day, around the time us kids got home from school, Mom would be gone to the Resurrection parish community hall to teach a bunch of kids religion class for an hour. Our instructions were to stay inside and do our homework until she got home.

The problem for us kids was that Raul used to work an early shift that saw him begin his workday at seven in the morning and end it at three. He didn't work too far from home, so he was usually home by three thirty or so, around the time we got home from school. Meanwhile, Mom's formal class time usually ended around three thirty, but she always stayed an hour or two later every afternoon to correct the kids' homework, or to prepare her lesson plan for the next day, or any other reason she could devise to stay away from Raul for as long as possible. She would manage to make it home by five-thirty or so, in time to make dinner. But by then, the damage was done.

By "damage" I mean that Raul took this opportunity while he had us in his grip to set us down on the living room sofa and "talk" to us. We called it "Raul's lectures." He would rant at us about all the things we were doing wrong, and all the things we should be doing, and all the ways that we were problems, and on and on and on.

We could not talk back to him. We could not say a word. We could not leave. He had us in his death grip, a captive, powerless audience, and he lectured us like this for an hour or two every afternoon, for several years, from the time I was about nine years old till I got into high school at age fourteen. Our friends would call on the phone, and he would answer and tell them we couldn't talk; we were busy.

It was horribly remarkable how much he had to complain about to us. A couple of hours every day, five days every week, for almost five years. It was a prison sentence. I retain nothing of what he said. I only remember how awful it felt. I only remember to this day how much more it turned me against him.

Mom knew what we had to endure so she could escape this awful man. We told her often enough. We told her what he said to us. But she did nothing. She abandoned us to this mean man. She left us, Jo Ann and me, to fend for ourselves. She was complicit in this act of verbal abuse and domestic terrorism.

She had adopted the attitude of "every man for himself." I hated her for that almost as much as I hated Raul. Ironic that she abandoned us to Raul in this way, for the sake of teaching other kids the principles of Christian love. Charity begins at home, I had always heard.

Raul was just as brutal and vicious as my father was in marking Sonny and me as "his territory." Flashback to shortly after Raul and Mom got married. Sonny and I had not been circumcised when we were born. I have no idea why, but that was the simple fact.

When Raul came into the picture, he managed to convince Mom that we should be circumcised, and somehow, she and our doctor ended up agreeing to this hideous mutilation on two grown boys, one barely eight years old, the other one almost twelve and, most likely, already in puberty.

I remember we went to Queen of Angels Hospital on Bellevue near Echo Park in Los Angeles. I remember Sonny and I shared the room together. I remember going under the anesthesia. I remember the pain afterward whenever the nurses came in to clean our wounds, and I remember how much it hurt when I had to pee. Sonny and I never talked about it at all. Ever.

As I got older, I came to understand that this was an act of violence at the most primal and personal level that Raul inflicted on my brother and me. It was one way in which he intended to beat us into subservience, just as he had attacked my mother. Of course, we only developed a crushing hatred of the man for this and all the other wounds and abuse he willfully inflicted on us all.

Over the years, whenever my dad came to take Sonny and me for the day, Jo Ann was never included. My dad refused to take her with us. We never understood it at the time, but we later learned that it was because my dad knew Jo Ann was Ernie's child, and he wanted nothing to do with her. My dad was small and stingy and jealous in his own way, just like Raul.

I remember crying and crying as I sat in the back seat looking out the window of the car, while Dad drove us away from the house. I wanted Jo Ann to come, too, and I couldn't understand why we had to leave her, and Jo Ann and Mom would be there, outside at the street, waving, Mom holding Jo Ann's hand while she was crying her little eyes out, as I was, she calling my name as I called out to her.

I will watch over you always had always been the way I felt for my little sister. Just like the picture on the wall of the little boy and girl with the guardian angel nearing the edge of the cliff. Raul tried his best to bend us to his will, but he never did break us. My dad did the minimal he could get away with to be a father, but it was all worthless. My guardian angel worked hard for me.

Jo Ann

Aftƒer I retired and moved to Italy, my dream was to live out my days "under the Tuscan sun," living *la dolce vita*. I applied for and was granted a permanent resident visa by the Italian government, allowing me free travel throughout the European Union. I was enjoying a life of travel throughout the Continent, where all the great capitals are less than one hundred dollars and a two-hour flight from Rome. I love to travel, always have, and for me, my time had come. My villa was very comfortable in a beautiful setting, I was an hour from Rome by train, and I very soon settled into a life of which many people can only dream.

But of course, plans are what we do, and life is what happens. Two years after I moved to Italy, it became clear that I needed to return home, as I described earlier. So I packed up my belongings and returned to the States. First to San Francisco to do volunteer work canvassing for the midterm 2018 elections, then to Eureka where my family lives. I settled into life in Eureka, in a nice apartment next door to my sister, Jo Ann.

I had always presumed, when I returned to the States, that the decision was mine and mine alone. I had my reasons for coming home, and it seemed clear that it was the right decision for me at the time. Soon, however, things began happening that made me realize that, once again, the unseen hand was at work, behind the scenes, directing our lives, even when we have no idea what is happening, and much less why.

Eight months after my return home, my niece Leslie, the daughter of my sister, Jo Ann, received a diagnosis of lung cancer, and the prognosis was not good. We were just beginning to get our minds around this horrific news, when, six weeks after she was diagnosed, Leslie passed away, overcome by the cancer that had metastasized beyond control. Words cannot describe the pain and anguish of this sudden, terrible event that upended our lives. Losing a child has been called the "unbearable grief" for a parent. We were all devastated.

JO ANN

Nine months after Leslie was taken from us, Jo Ann's husband, Mike, was killed in an accident on his motorcycle on the highway not far from home. It would do no good to attempt to describe what this has been like. I can do no honor to their memories by saying any more.

I can only say that it was a good thing that I was here, by my dear sister's side, to render, as best as anyone can, some small measure of comfort to her under these awful conditions. I cannot imagine if I had been halfway on the other side of the world when these horrible disasters struck. I may have believed when I returned to the States that it was for my own reasons, that I was in control of my destiny. But now I know, beyond any doubt, that I was meant to be here, for the little comfort it may have afforded my sister.

I cannot say why these two beautiful people were taken from us with no warning. My faith allows me only a small comfort in presuming there is some master plan. But I dare not tell Jo Ann that the unseen hand of our Creator is at work here for some good reason as yet unclear to us mere mortals. That would be smug and condescending to the point of cruelty, and I see no good that could possibly come of it.

And I cannot in this situation see that image on my mother's wall of the angel standing close by, protecting the little boy and girl (whom I had always imagined to be my sister and I) and keeping us from harm's way, saying: *I will watch over you always.*

This is the place where faith has to take over. Otherwise, despair rushes in to fill the sickening void.

Requiem for a Stranger

I HAD A DREAM ABOUT my father once. When I awoke, I was gasping hard for breath—huge, heaving spasms that wracked my lungs. I bolted upright, desperately sucking for air that would not come. I felt like I was drowning. Tears soaked the pillow under my head. My heart was pounding.

In this dream, I was standing at a door, pounding hard on the door, and I knew, somehow, that my father was on the other side, waiting for me. I could sense that he needed my help, but I was helpless to do anything for him. I waited, pounding, waiting for release, from the dream, from the waiting, for freedom, for something I know not what. I waited and pounded for an eternity.

Then, suddenly, the door flew open toward me and my father was there, looking as shocked as I was to be there, and he looked a mess. He was wrapped in bandages on his arms and legs. He was bent forward, in obvious pain, and appeared very weak. The years were etched deeply in his face. He was old, frail, a man I barely recognized. I man I barely knew.

He stumbled across the threshold and fell into my arms. I held him close. His weakness made me stronger as I clutched this man I never knew. It mattered not that he never cared for me. The years he let slip by without a call or a visit were unimportant to me now. A lifetime in which he never made the effort meant nothing to me in this moment. All that mattered was that we were here, and I wanted to take him away from this place, and I felt that our long and lonely estrangement was, at last, over.

Here he was, finally, I thought to myself, and I would take him home with me. I struggled to find the words to tell him: *I will watch over you always.*

That's when I woke up crying as hard as I have ever cried in my life.

Crying because we were together or because we never were—I knew not, I cared not. The only thing I felt was a sense of reconciliation in my heart. And on my lips lingered a question I could not find the words to say and was just getting ready to ask him: "My father, did you think about me at all as you lay on your deathbed?"

Adolescence

My teen years were fairly normal, despite the problems in my mother's marriage to Raul, the constant fighting, the ever-present lack of money, and the gradual descent of Sonny deeper into problems with the law. At the age of seventeen, Sonny was no longer living at home with us, after his one-year stint at San Dimas.

That didn't break Sonny's spirit but only hardened it, as is so often the case with many of those who emerge from the criminal justice system. When he got out, he took up again with his old buddies, in direct violation of parole. But he didn't care. By the time he announced he was moving in with his girlfriend, our house itself seemed to breathe a sigh of relief.

It was the sixties, and I was a typical teenager. The Beatles, the Rolling Stones, the whole British invasion had taken America and the world by storm. My sister and I wore out our rock-and-roll albums playing them every chance we could.

I excelled in high school, joining drama club, where I performed in some plays and became assistant stage manager. I joined the journalism club, where I became assistant editor of the school newspaper. I signed up for extracurricular Latin class, joined band and played tenor saxophone, marching in formation at high school football games and performing in school concerts and regional competitions.

I even joined a garage band: "Thee Realistics—*with Thee Real Sound*" it said on our business cards. I was elected student body secretary. I took a job after school at a gas station and then at the local Dairy Queen. Through it all, I continued getting straight As and was a constant name on the dean's list after every report card.

There was no particular event or episode during these years that I recall—like the ball of green yarn—as irrefutable evidence that my guardian angel was watching over me. Suffice it to say, I am confident that she most likely had my back to make sure I did not get too close to danger, for my life was filled with joy and positive energy and good friends who shared with me an excitement for learning and productive endeavors. I am also certain that she was there, constantly encouraging me to stay on my path of discovery and growth and maturity.

It was a happy time in my life personally, I was popular among my friends, and the days always seemed long and filled with new joys. But I do recall that life was hell for my mom in her constant struggles with Raul. I was not oblivious to her marital difficulties, but I had my own life to live. Her marital problems kept her from being a loving, supportive, encouraging mother. She was too consumed with the anger and stress between Sonny and Raul.

Mom was, however, always glad that I got such good grades, because it saved her money. In my Catholic high school, the students who ranked summa cum laude for the semester got their tuition free of charge the following semester, and Mom did like this benefit that my grades brought to the household budget. She also took a share of my hard-earned money from my after-school jobs.

My mom was defined throughout her life by a state of want. Money for her was always a struggle and has remained so to this day. My mother, in her penury, in her constant hand-wringing and anxiety over the lack of money, taught me by example of what I never wanted to experience or how I never wanted to be, even if times were tight.

The word *penury* may seem too harsh a word to describe our lives. Poverty is the word that defines the state of being poor or indigent; while penury describes extreme want leading to destitution. The difference is understood, and I do not use the word penury lightly. It's true that we always had food on the table and a roof over our heads. Mom did always manage to put us kids through parochial school, which cost money. The welfare system and the social safety net, such as it was at the time, did work for us. We were never homeless, nor did we ever starve.

But for my mother, penury was more like a state of mind, a destitution of spirit, in the sense that the hyperawareness of want was always a dominant, controlling theme in our home. My mother lived and breathed a sense of lack. She was always talking about money, how to get more, how to spend less, how often we outgrew our clothes, and how much our ravenous little appetites wreaked havoc on her budget. She made us feel like a burden on her soul.

I have vivid memories of her sitting at the kitchen table for hours on end writing up endless drafts of monthly budgets. She would look over the bills and prioritize them over and over again, shuffling them front to back and then back again, as if this act of moving the bills around would tire them out and they would give up and walk away. It was difficult not to notice that we were poor, and that's a heavy burden to put on a sensitive kid with no control over such matters.

This is the reason I can easily remember how much Sonny's trench coat cost (twenty dollars) and how it compared to our monthly rent (eighty dollars). To this day, I can tell you how much money we spent every week (twenty dollars) on groceries in 1965 for our family of six (my mom and Raul soon had a daughter between them, Carol). Blue Chip and S&H green stamps were a valued commodity in our home.

I've already noted how Mom pushed me to get good grades in high school because I basically financed my own education. And while she would tell me that by taking some of the money I earned from my after-school jobs she was teaching me the value of a dollar, in truth, the only lesson I took from it was that I never wanted to be like her. I knew the value of money and what things cost. In that house, it was impossible not to know.

In high school, I read the short story by D. H. Lawrence "The Rocking-Horse Winner." In this story, the mother is in a constant state of anxiety and stress over never having enough money, even though her family is middle class and outwardly seems to be relatively comfortable. The mother is haunted by a sense of having no luck with money, and her anxiety permeates the household. Paul, her son, picks up his mother's stress and even claims that he can hear the house at night whispering: "There must be more money, there must be more money."

Paul has a rocking horse, and he rides his horse for hours and hours and works himself into a frenzied state of clairvoyance in which he is able to pick the winners at a nearby racetrack. He tells his uncle about his strange power to predict winners. The two of them begin betting real money at the races and winning, but it is never enough.

One day, Paul tells his uncle to bet on a longshot to win and rides his rocking horse harder and harder for many hours until he collapses and dies of fatigue. The horse Paul picked does win the race and brings in a huge amount of money. The mother is now rich at last, but she has lost her son to her maniacal craving for more money.

In my mother's house, poverty stalked us like a wild animal. It haunted us night and day like an angry ghost rattling its chains. It hung thick in the air like the smoke from the burning wreckage of our lives. My mother was emotionally bankrupt in her mind, from the inside out, and no amount of money would have made a difference.

In this regard, I believe my guardian angel diligently and protectively kept me on the good road so that I would not be plagued by this sense of such crushing want throughout my life. I believe my guardian angel was watching out for me in this important way. Indeed, once I was on my professional career path, the money came easy, and, aside from a few notable periods of struggle in my younger years that strengthened me and taught me some valuable lessons, I have been blessed with financial security and peace of mind for most of my adult life.

Vietnam and the Draft

I WAS TEN YEARS OLD when President John F. Kennedy began sending thousands of military advisors to Vietnam. By the time I was thirteen, a shooting war involving American troops was underway that wouldn't end until 1975, when I was twenty-four. Vietnam defined my life, my hopes, my dreams, and my greatest fears throughout my most formative years. It was the existential threat that was more direct and ever present to me and my cohorts than nuclear destruction even.

The nuns in grammar school were on top of this story from the start. Don't ask me how they knew. They were really quite prescient in their analysis of how it would all come down. I can remember, very clearly, Sister Mary Florentine in seventh grade constantly telling us that we would be going to Vietnam someday to fight communism.

We were just twelve years old. Heroic GIs in uniform fighting the bad guys was still a childhood fantasy of World War II movies, still being produced and fed to us. A rich diet of brave men fighting the good fight, jumping on grenades to save their comrades, sharpshooters picking Germans out of pillboxes on a beachhead, or sticking a bayonet into the Japanese soldier in the jungle.

None of my friends paid attention to Sister Florentine. We were busy trying to make sense of a radical new subject called "the new math"—polynomials, the number line, graphs. Yeah, right, Sister. What's your point? Or, don't be stupid, if America is involved, the war will be over in no time.

Fast-forward to draft age. I am eighteen years old, and I enroll in the Selective Service System. Meanwhile, the number of U.S. servicemen in Vietnam is at an all-time high of almost half a million men in combat. There seems no way out. My friends and I are scared to death. We may have to go fight. Those nuns, I thought. How did they know?

I had an innate pathological fear, an intuitive sense that I would not survive boot camp, much less combat duty, if I had to enlist or get drafted. I knew that I was not cut out for combat. I was the sensitive poet type.

Zero bravado. Tall and thin and strong, but very weak inside. I knew instinctively that, if I ended up in uniform, I would be shipped off to a combat zone in some base camp in-country and, soon thereafter, be shipped home in a body bag. I was grateful for the good grades that assured me a 2-S college student deferment.

Nevertheless, I worried, still, that this damn war just might continue indefinitely, still drafting kids my age when my deferment ended after college. In fact, the war did rage on for more than five years after I entered college, so I was not wrong in my dire assessment of the long-term problem facing me. Sister Mary Florentine's words rang louder with every year in that quagmire of war.

Then came the fall of 1969, draft age for me and my first semester in college when the first draft lottery took place. I remember all us boys sitting in the campus dining hall at dinnertime, listening to the overhead radio broadcasting the results of the lottery. As they drew one birthday at a time and called out the number, guys at the head of the list would scream in fear and anger, certain now that they would be called up into the army, once they lost their deferment.

That system kept a lot of boys working hard in school, fretting over keeping good grades as if their lives depended on it. Their lives did depend on it. I have never prayed harder in my life for a lottery number that would ensure my safety.

The voice from Washington, DC, on the radio droned on and on as the evening turned to dark on that cold December day. We were all well aware of the cutoff number—115. Any young man whose birthday appeared after lottery number 115 would not be called up in the draft, not that year, and not after leaving college. Eventually, the dining hall was filled not with boys crying or screaming or cursing but with the boys who were laughing and cheering their good fortune in the spinning wheel of death.

My draft number was 286. I would never be drafted, no matter how long we were at war, no matter how many were called up, no matter how many body bags came home. It may seem like a miracle of fate, a simple matter of the luck of the draw. But I know it was my guardian angel, always watching over me.

Stupid Stuff

I HAD ALWAYS EXCELLED IN school, and my professional career, for the most part, was a success productively and financially beyond my wildest dreams. I am grateful to a combination of factors and circumstances that came together for me; to people who saw something in me and gave me the opportunities that I made the most of at the right time; to the intersection of external forces and internal preparations that put me in good positions; and, of course, to my guardian angel who has always protected me from harm or pointed me in the right direction. Thank you, all. To say that I accomplished all those things without anyone's help would be blatantly wrong and patently stupid.

Despite all the good things that I have done or that came my way, there are many notable exceptions that I own fully, totally, and solely. I admit that I have done a lot of stupid things in my life, things I am ashamed of, things I regret even still, things I have no one to blame for but myself. An honest and open telling here would not be complete if I omit these stories from the narrative.

In my early twenties, I was not in a good place. I was the father of a beautiful daughter, but I had left her and her mother because I was immature and not capable of owning up to my responsibilities. This bad behavior on my part did a lot of damage to all of us, and I will always be grateful to my daughter for accepting my apologies and forgiving me as she has. I am working on making up for lost time and repairing the damage I did to her when I was stupid. She is a mother herself now, and I am the proud grandfather of a beautiful young girl.

One of the idiot things I regret doing in my twenties was to get arrested for smuggling pot into the country from Mexico. It was a harrowing experience, one that I learned from and never repeated again. It was another situation where I can only say that my guardian angel delivered me from the worst possible outcome.

It could have been much worse for me than it turned out to be. It's possible I could have ended up in the federal penitentiary for a very long time. *I will watch over you always.* "Even when you do stupid stuff," I might add to her words.

After leaving my young wife, Carmen, and my one-year-old daughter, Aimee Vanessa, I moved to Arizona to "find myself." My life was in shambles. I was drifting badly. I had dropped out of college after trying to make a go of it as a young father; the college that I had worked so hard for all of my high school years, the college where I had had a full scholarship for four years, including housing and a living stipend. My high school grades and SAT scores had served me well. It was a shame I blew all that in one night of teenage sex, but that's how it was, and I learned long ago not to look back on what has been lost or what might have been.

I lived in a stunning place in Arizona, on the outskirts of Flagstaff, at the base of beautiful and majestic Humphrey's Peak, over 12,000 feet of dormant volcanic cinder cone in a ring of similar mountains known as the San Francisco Peaks. It is a sacred mountain to both the Hopi and the Dineh (Navajo). The Dineh name for it is Dook'o'oosliid. No one who has ever looked up at that amazing ring of long-dormant volcanoes can deny its power and preeminence over the landscape of the local geography and the landscape of the soul. I went there to make connection with the soul of my ancestors, to find my spiritual legacy.

I lived in a sprawling, old ranch house with three other guys. This house was once the home of the original owner of the huge ranch in the great valley surrounding us. It was called Bader Ranch, in the place known as Fort Valley, elevation 7,500 feet.

I spent many wonderful times getting to know this amazing land. I was constantly taking trips up to the sacred peaks that towered above me. A good road went up the peaks to a ski resort called the Arizona Snowbowl, elevation 9,200 feet. From there, you could ride a ski lift another 2,000 feet. Then, it's a relatively easy walk up to the very peak of Mt. Humphries at 12,637 feet. The trip took about four hours total from my house to the top of the peak.

In the summertime, I would often do this trip alone with nothing but a small daypack filled with some food, binoculars, a flashlight, and my sleeping bag. I would spend the night there, waking up in the middle of a dream to find the stars so close I felt that I could reach up and touch them. Or there were times when I would drive to the Grand Canyon, another Native sacred place just an hour away, and spend a few days there camping at the South Rim.

It was a good place and a good time in which to get away from myself, from my past, from the mistakes I had made when I became a father, then abandoned my daughter. I fooled myself into believing that I had escaped my past by moving to this idyllic setting away from civilization. But the quiet nights under the stunning canopy of the Milky Way and the crystalline blue skies filled with sunshine only brought into high relief the quiet hell that tormented my soul.

I had very little money and no means of support. There were not a lot of jobs in Flagstaff for someone with no experience in anything. Flagstaff was a college town, home to Northern Arizona University, and competition was fierce for the lowest entry-level jobs. I got by on the small bit of savings I had brought with me when I began this adventure. But eventually, the money ran out.

I had met a guy, Steve, at a bar in Flagstaff named Shakey Drake's. Steve was a bit older than I, and we would get together now and then to have a beer and smoke pot. We were both always broke and usually had to hit up his friends for beer money or to bum a joint or two. It was a miserable life in so many ways. I have never been lower nor felt so bad about myself.

One day, Steve and I got the bright idea of driving across the border into Mexico several hours south of us, to buy cheap pot and take it back to Flagstaff where we would make a "killing" selling to the local college students. Brilliant. So we scraped together what little cash we had and got in my car, an old mustard-colored Toyota two-door coupe, filled up the tank, and headed south down beautiful Highway 89.

We made it to Nogales, Arizona, where we crossed the border. We stayed in a cheap motel on the Mexican side and turned in for the night. Next day, we walked around town until we found some Mexican guy who looked like he might know something. We ended up making a plan to meet him later that afternoon to buy two kilos of weed. I don't recall the arithmetic, but we weren't going to make as much money as we had originally thought. No matter, at least we would have weed for ourselves.

The next day, we headed north to the border crossing. The border agent took one look at us and motioned for us to pull over. The agents began a systematic check of my car, and it didn't take them long to find the weed. They cuffed us both and took us inside for processing. We were put in separate rooms where we were questioned individually. Then, we were booked and put in separate holding cells. It was Friday, I remember, and the judge would hear our case on Monday and make a preliminary decision at that time.

It was awful. I won't go into detail about the conditions in the cell or my state of mind. One thing I will say is that my predicament very quickly became very scary. The public defender came in to meet me that first day after I had been in detention for a few hours. A guard came in and handcuffed me, and I was led out into the conference room where my attorney could talk over my case with me.

The first thing he did was to ask me to tell him about the heroin. Heroin? Heroin? I suddenly felt faint and nauseous and felt the blood simultaneously drain from my body and make me cold, then rush back into my head and make me hot. The attorney himself blanched when he saw my reaction.

It turns out that Steve had made a side deal with the Mexican who sold us the pot. Steve was a junkie, something I was not aware of. Steve had bought a stash of heroin for himself, it was in his pocket, and the guards had found it when they frisked Steve.

The public defender was now telling me that we could both get sent up not just for transporting two kilos of pot across the border for sale and distribution, no small problem in itself, but also for possession of heroin, which carried a maximum penalty of ten years in prison with time off for good behavior. I saw my life flash before my eyes. My life was over. I was so stupid, it hurts even today to think about it. I spent that weekend in jail dazed and in a comatose state of shock. I had the dry heaves for hours.

Monday afternoon finally came. I felt like I was walking up the scaffold for my beheading as the guard marched me in handcuffs to the judge chambers. It was not a typical courtroom scene. This was a pretty cut-and-dried straight-up deliberation. The proceedings moved along, and the public defender made my plea of guilty. The judge spent some time asking my attorney a few things I no longer recall. The minutes ticked by like hours. I felt sick the whole time.

The judge finally closed my file and asked me to stand up while he announced his decision. The public defender helped me to my feet. I looked at the judge, the tears streaming down my face. The judge said that it was clear that I had no idea about the heroin and that I was innocent of this charge. Steve had a prior conviction for heroin possession, and I had had nothing on me. The judge also noted that I seemed young and immature and foolish to undertake a stupid venture like this. I nodded my head in agreement, the tears dropping in a flood on the worn carpet at my feet.

The judge said he would sentence me to time served (three days in that cell), a five-hundred-dollar fine, impoundment of my vehicle, and probation for five years. If I stayed out of trouble anywhere in the U.S. (this was a federal crime I had committed), I could clear my record in five years, since I was being charged as a minor. My twenty-first birthday was just a few days away. It would have gone much harder for me if it had happened less than a week later.

I had a girlfriend back in Los Angeles at the time, and she drove out to Nogales to pick me up and pay my fine. When I got out of jail, we drove up to Flagstaff where I packed my stuff and returned to L.A. I moved in with my girlfriend, got a job, and paid her the money she had put up for my fine.

Five years later, I went through the legal process to expunge my record. I never learned what became of Steve and never cared to. It was years before I returned to Flagstaff. Arizona is beautiful, and I have been there often for its remarkable natural wonders. It is the land where my father was born. The land where my innocence died.

I will watch over you always—words I took to heart, words I always believed, words that never seemed to fail me. Even when I did stupid stuff.

The Near-Fatal Collision

My Uncle Ray was nearing death in Los Angeles, and my mother called to tell us we should come see him in the hospital. Uncle Ray had had a rough life since the day he was shot by a madman in his apartment while celebrating the birthday of his best friend.

The madman killed my uncle's best friend, Lalo, and my uncle's wife, and blew several bullets into Uncle Ray's brain, a couple of which the doctors were never able to remove. The only reason Lalo's wife didn't suffer the same fate is because she was in the bathroom at the time and out of the line of fire.

The short version of this story is that my Uncle Ray and the others were at Ray's apartment in Hawthorne drinking and having fun on Lalo's birthday. The landlord lived in one of the units and became annoyed and came over to complain about the noise they were making.

The revelers didn't think too much of his request and apparently ignored him and went on drinking and partying. The landlord left, then returned sometime later with his rifle and several magazine clips and pounded on the door. When my uncle opened the door this time, the landlord put a violent end to the festivities and to two lives, and changed my uncle's life forever.

I remember the night this happened when all of us were at the hospital. I remember my uncle in his bed all bandaged up, his face swollen and purple, semiconscious and delirious. I remember he was strapped to the rails of the hospital bed, and he kept rapping his knuckles on the rails and saying to no one in particular: "Honey, bring me a drink, wouldja honey, I'm dying of thirst here."

We were told by the nurses that this was the drugs talking through him. He was being sufficiently hydrated intravenously. My own theory was that this may have been the last thing he was saying to his wife before the bullets took their lives and took away his rational thought.

THE NEAR-FATAL COLLISION

For many years, my uncle had a long, slow, and painful rehabilitation, hardly a rehabilitation, which never fully restored him to his prior state. He had poor vision, he had constant headaches, he could never stop talking about that night, he could never keep his hands steady enough to hold down any kind of job. Uncle Ray had been an electronics engineer in the aerospace industry, with an excellent mind and fine motor skills, valued for his precision touch and his quick mind. But now, he just sat around endlessly chain-smoking cigarettes, drinking cheap beer, watching TV all day, and trying to make sense of his shattered world.

He lived (if you can call it that) in this gradually worsening state of decay for perhaps another fifteen years. He was in and out of the hospital for various related ailments. The long list of compounding health problems took their toll over time on his body and his mind until, eventually, he ended up in the hospital for the last time.

I believed he willed himself to die, after having had enough of a life that seemed to be no life at all. I never talked to him about this, but I have to wonder if he ever wished that the bullet had put an end to him as well, along with everything else he held dear in his life.

On the day my mother told us we should come to the hospital for the last time, Jo Ann was living in Eureka and I was in San Francisco. Jo Ann already had been planning to go to Los Angeles on this particular weekend for a hair show. Jo Ann was a hairdresser and she and some coworkers were going to a big West Coast business convention. We agreed that they would stop in San Francisco on their way south, pick me up in the morning, and we would go from there.

They had been driving since very early in the predawn hours, and when they got to my place, I took over the driving. We had one stop yet before getting on Interstate 5 for the six-hour drive to Southern California. There was one other hairdresser friend we had to pick up at her home in Fremont.

In Fremont, Jo Ann's friend got in the car, and I drove us out of town to the interstate. The road out of Fremont was a narrow, two-lane country road that crossed a wide, dry creek bed. Thick concrete abutments flanked either side of the bridge just before the bridge spanned the wide creek bed. I was driving the twenty-five-mph speed limit, it was eight o'clock on a Saturday morning, and the others in the car were beginning to settle in and catch up on sleep for the long drive. Jo Ann sat in the front with me, and we made small talk as we started on our journey.

I looked up in the rearview mirror and I saw a large blue tow truck barreling down on us from behind, quickly looming larger and larger in the mirror. The driver in my rearview mirror was clearly in a very big hurry and driving at a reckless high speed. I looked to the road ahead where it narrowed on the bridge, and I saw a long line of cars approaching at a slow and leisurely pace, driving into town from the neighboring countryside, probably on their way to the mall or the farmers' market or some other Saturday morning shopping errands.

The big blue tow truck was now right on my tail and not slowing down, and then I saw him make a stupid move to pass me up. He cut into the lane right in the path of this oncoming line of cars, all of them oblivious to the scene that I had been tracking for the last thirty seconds or so.

The tow truck did not alter course, nor did he slow down and get back behind me. I decided I should get out of the way so he could veer into our lane and out of the line of traffic still nonchalantly coming closer to disaster. The sun was behind me, in their eyes, so that first driver may not have fully realized what was heading his way. I pulled over to my right just before the concrete abutment on the bridge, on what little shoulder remained before the road became a bridge with no shoulder.

The tow truck kept right on going, fast as ever, trying to beat the oncoming traffic, and as we all sat there watching this slow-motion catastrophe unfolding before our eyes, the truck driver realized his mistake and careened to the right of the road, desperately trying to get out of the way of the oncoming traffic.

But it was too late. The tow truck driver hit the first car on the car's left front corner and sent it spinning full circle till it faced the second car behind him, which then hit him head-on. The tow truck was not finished moving, and we saw it hit another oncoming car as that car tried to swerve out of the way of the first two stricken vehicles. The driver behind that swerving car hit his brakes, and the car behind him plowed into him from behind.

Meanwhile, the impact of the tow truck on the first vehicle dislodged the giant spare tire that had been chained to the back of the tow truck. It was a tow truck that hauls big rig tractor trailers on the interstate, and the spare tire that it had been carrying was for eighteen-wheeler trucks, much, much larger than a car tire.

That huge spare tire went flying through the air and headed straight for us now as we were stopped right behind it. The tire was flipping end over end,

THE NEAR-FATAL COLLISION

just like you would flip a quarter in the air and watch it flip over and over on its way to the ground. The tire was beginning to make its descent, and the trajectory seemed to put it squarely on the roof of our car.

We sat in our car, helpless, speechless, unable to move, nowhere to go, cars blocking us from behind, the wreckage of cars before us, the tow truck crashed into the side of the bridge and steaming radiator water, and that giant tire looming larger and larger, spinning over and over toward us, on its trajectory of destruction.

Then something truly bizarre happened. Nothing. Nothing happened. The tire went sailing right over the roof of our car. It seemed to move in slow motion, so I can only assume massive amounts of adrenaline were pumping through my body. The huge heavy tire missed us completely, went right over the top of us, and landed squarely on the car behind us on the bridge. That roof was all crushed in, the windshield shattered and pieces flying in every direction. I saw all this through the rearview mirror.

But we were safe. We were delivered from a fate I can only ponder. Jo Ann and I looked at each other, and I moved us into place and slowly drove us out of that path of destruction toward the other side of the bridge across the dry creek bed. We picked our way through the wreckage on the road.

People were injured. At least six cars were smashed up. The tow truck driver stumbled out of the cab of his truck, onto the asphalt, bleeding from his head and stumbling around in a daze. I could hear people screaming, calling out, I saw radiators steaming, fluids pouring out from under several vehicles. A scene of carnage and destruction on such a beautiful warm spring morning. I guess fate cares not for the serene state of the natural world at hand and merely makes its way through our lives regardless.

We could not stop. We had to get to Los Angeles. My uncle's death was imminent. We drove slowly through the wreckage; some of us turned our heads away. I kept my eyes fixed on the road before me. We came off the bridge on the other side and onto the road leading to the interstate.

Before we got to the interstate on-ramp, I pulled into a rest stop, and we all got out to shake off the grip of fear that clung to us still. I went into the bathroom and had the dry heaves for several minutes. I splashed cold water on my face, and when I looked in the mirror, I saw my guardian angel standing there behind me.

The rest of the drive was in a daze. I remember very little of it. The humming sound of our tires on the highway. The sunlight in its long, slow arc moving the shadows from east to west across our field of vision. Each of us in our own way losing track of time, reliving those awful moments when our day began.

When we got to Los Angeles, I called the highway patrol and told them what we had seen. I told them we would make a statement, but I was told it was not necessary, there were plenty of witnesses. I was told the tow truck driver was drunk and that two people had lost their lives that morning, while several more were seriously injured. They took my name and number and told me they would call me if they needed my testimony, but they never did call. My uncle died the next day, after we visited him for the last time.

Jo Ann and I have relived that experience and talked it through many times in the years since. We both recall the same thing, drawing from the same shared memory. And although I have seen the power of my guardian angel manifest to me and me alone in many ways through the years, this was the only time in my life where I had felt my guardian angel was doing her faithful duty for both my sister and me at the same time and in the same dangerous situation, just like the angel protecting that little boy and girl in the picture on the wall in my mother's bedroom in the projects, telling us both: *I will watch over you always.*

My Professional Career

No one could have predicted the circuitous and intertwining route my family history, education, and work experience would take to bring me to the most significant accomplishment of my professional career—an accomplishment that also stands as a major and historic event in American Indian community development.

It is an achievement that has the hand of my guardian angel all over it. And her efforts on my behalf in this achievement go back a long time, and they go very deep. I shake my head even now when I think about the energy and the planning and the patience that my guardian angel put into making all this happen. She certainly outdid herself this time.

I always had a natural talent for writing, and I felt that I could hear my calling from a very early age. By the age of eleven, I was writing poetry, and reading poets and writers of all kinds. By the time I got into high school, I knew I wanted to be a writer. By the time I graduated, I had decided that I would get a college degree majoring in English, teach high school English, and write the great American novel, or poetry, or something.

My college career was derailed when Carmen and I got pregnant, and I went through what I call my "lost years," drifting, working at dumb jobs to pay the rent, and pretty much demoralized and wasting time. I was living in Virginia and working for the park service in the 1970s. After a few years, I got my act together again and returned to college, where I majored in English. At last, my great childhood dream was once again on track.

I graduated college and moved to San Francisco. I began to look around at the job prospects for someone with an English degree and a talent for the written word. I landed a job as an account executive in a public relations agency, put my skills to work there, and made very good money. Much more than teaching, I was pleased to note.

I worked in public relations for several years, moving up the corporate ladder, making big bucks, and playing to my strengths. It was a good time. I felt that those few years that I had gotten sidetracked were behind me now, and I was well on my way to a successful career. I was writing feature articles for magazines on the side and getting satisfaction from that work as well.

Then, in 1986, Sonny died of a heroin overdose, and my world fell apart. I took his death real hard. Alex had overdosed many years earlier, and I began to worry about that "curse of the Moisas" that my father talked about so often. Was this curse embedded in our DNA? I had unrealistic fears. I was haunted by horrible nightmares constantly. I could not hold myself together. Work was stressful and overwhelming. I decided I needed a break to pull myself together. I quit working and took time out for myself.

I spent the next year pouring my anxieties into the creative process. I wrote a fictional screenplay based loosely on the story of Ruben Salazar, a Mexican American journalist in East Los Angeles murdered by the L.A. County Sheriff's Department. I put a lot of personal history about myself and Sonny in it. It served as a purging and a cleansing, and it did some good. It was a catharsis that offered me a respite from the trauma I had been going through. I was starting to find my center again.

When I had finished the screenplay and began shopping it around, I decided I also needed to do something outside the home for my sense of well-being. So I volunteered to do mundane clerk work at an American Indian nonprofit organization in the Bay Area. It was an organization that worked to place American Indian orphans in the foster homes of American Indian parents. It felt like a good way to close the loop on my own experience as an infant foundling, a way to help others who had been abandoned like me. Things were beginning to come together for me once again, little by little. By this time, Sonny had been dead almost two years.

One day, the organization where I volunteered had a grant deadline coming, and they asked if I could help them out. The work was close enough to what I had done writing marketing proposals in my public relations career, so I agreed to give it a shot. Although we didn't get the grant, it dawned on me that here was a need for my writing and proposal organizing skills in the nonprofit world. I began writing grant proposals for another American Indian organization that could afford me at full-time salary. Before long, I was bringing in big bucks for this organization.

I was instrumental in building a Bay Area-wide, urban Indian community development plan. I spent two years in the organization piloting this effort, and I raised $650,000 to implement the pilot projects that we had established in the planning phase. This amount of grant money from private philanthropy was unheard of in the American Indian nonprofit world. Most of the local urban Indian organizations operated on one dedicated federal grant, maybe a smaller state community development block grant. They were also at risk of federal cutbacks. They were largely unknown to the philanthropic community of foundations. I had changed all that. Now we were known to the Bay Area foundation world.

After a few years, I decided to set myself up as an independent contractor, specializing in grant proposals for a variety of local American Indian nonprofits. I had hit upon a great idea, working from home, for several clients at a time, having the flexibility and the independence to call my own shots. I flourished in this freer structure, and I made a very good living bringing in lots of money for my clients. I had found my niche, and I had a large market all to myself. No one else was doing anything like this.

Soon enough, my reputation and good work caught the attention of the executive director of Friendship House Association of American Indians, a nonprofit in San Francisco that operated a residential alcohol and drug treatment center for homeless American Indians. The organization had dreamed of buying property in San Francisco and building a larger facility to treat more people in need.

It was a good idea whose time had come. For over thirty years, Friendship House had been renting the building where they treated clients. The rent was always going up. As was an ever-growing need for their services.

The organization did excellent work, and referrals were coming from all over Indian country and from local treatment programs that were taking in Native American homeless and addicted people who were coming in off the streets of San Francisco and the entire Bay Area. Friendship House treated clients in a Native-based, wholistic treatment modality. The clients responded well to this unique methodology, and the success rate was exceptionally high as a result.

The director asked me if I would help them try to get this project off the ground. They had been dreaming about this acquisition and expansion for years, and she felt that I stood the best chance of success. Although I didn't have any direct experience in developing real estate, I told her I would give it a try. The rest, as they say, is history.

Within three years, I had raised more than $3 million and a commitment to support the project from the mayor of San Francisco and the board of supervisors, and we had purchased the ideal site for the project. I had acquired the services of an architectural firm to design the facility, and I had lined up all the neighborhood and community support and linkages vital to ensuring the project's completion, a beautiful, three-story structure that ultimately came in at a price tag of $12 million.

At this point in the project, the actual development of the site required highly technical project management skills far beyond my abilities or experience, and I secured the services of a qualified consulting firm that could carry the ball over the goal line. I stepped aside and let the housing development experts take it from there, while I took a secondary role raising additional grant funds for capital and for the expanded services that would be necessary once the new facility was built and filled with clients.

I am especially proud to note that among my efforts for Friendship House, I secured a federal earmark, a line-item allocation of $250,000 in the congressional budget for 2005. The Friendship House name was actually listed in the federal budget. I had written the grant request and worked with Nancy Pelosi's office for about eighteen months, and then it happened.

In appreciation for my efforts, Pelosi gave me four autographed passes to the special viewing area at our nation's capital on President Barack Obama's first inauguration in January 2009, plus she gave us passes to attend a private reception for Obama and his wife. I took Jo Ann and Mike, and together with my wife we spent a glorious week living four blocks from the Capitol Building and had a wonderful time attending the inauguration. It was an amazing experience. We believed in those heady days of Obama, that America had finally come around, and that a new era was at hand. Yes, we can, we all proudly exclaimed. Hope.

In a few years, the new Friendship House was completed, and my work was done. It was nothing short of a miracle. I had done something that everyone had said was impossible to do. Friendship House was now the operator and owner of a major residential treatment facility serving American Indians, one of only three in the entire country that was Indian-owned and operated. It was the high-water mark of my career, my crowning achievement. For the first three years I had been the only one working at this effort, and I had done everything that had to be done to get it off the ground and help the board of directors to finally realize their long-time dream.

Throughout my work with Friendship House, I was guided and motivated by the realization that here was an opportunity to do something to help homeless Indians overcome addiction to drugs and alcohol. I began every morning with a prayer to Sonny and Alex, asking them to help me in this difficult, demanding, and important work.

It was an opportunity that came to me, out of the blue, and it immediately resonated deep within my soul. I did not go looking for this work. It found me. When the director first approached and asked me to take on this project, she told me she had absolute faith in me; that if I couldn't make it happen, no one could.

How could my unique set of skills, personal history, and timing align in such a way as to successfully bring about such a massive effort? It's not a project I had ever planned to do. It just appeared magically, the confluence of many disparate things at the right time. I thank my guardian angel for setting me long ago on the path that ended up here. In a place where it seems I was always meant to be.

From this vantage point in my advanced years, life to me now seems like a great sea voyage. We catch the tide out of safe harbor and set sail on our adventure.

Along the way we chart a course, but not every destination is within our control. The winds may turn against us, or our sails may lie limp for days and days in a listless eddy. The current may pull us this way or that, or the stars that guide us by night may cloud over. Much of the time, we float alone on open water, no one to connect with. Nothing visible as far as the eye can see.

Then one day, we see land looming ahead on the distant horizon. We make our way for shore. Who knows what lies ahead? Only the wreckage of other ships, other hopes, other destinies can offer a warning to us along the way; but we, we alone, captain our own ship toward our makeshift dream of uncertain good fortune

From this perspective now, it has become abundantly clear to me that everything in my education, professional career, and family history was pointing in this direction. It is one of the clearest manifestations of the unseen hand of our Creator working over a very long time (from our perspective) to make this project happen. *I will watch over you always.* I remember the words of Stevie Wonder in the song "As." He sings that God has placed us exactly where we need to be, even though we may feel otherwise.

The Insidious Scar Tissue of Racism

IN BEAUTY I WILL walk. My father was born to a man of mixed Native heritage, including Navajo and Tohono O'odham, and a Mexican American mother. He was born in Arizona, not far from his ancestral homelands, yet he never cared to venture into the territory of his heritage, Dinetah, the land of the Navajo.

My father, from what little I know of him, never cared much for his Native ancestry. He left Arizona for Los Angeles at an early age under circumstances I do not know. He never grew up in his Native culture. He never spoke his Native tongue. He became, for all intents and purposes, just another Mexican American in East Los Angeles. He was happy that he could "pass" for Mexican American. It was a step up from being Indian in Arizona, in those days when being Indian in Arizona was only a step up from being a dog.

My mother, who was born in Los Angeles of Mexican American parents, learned Spanish at home. My mother was Mexican American in Los Angeles at a time when Mexican American was a bad word. When we were kids, she absolutely refused to teach us Spanish, even when we asked her to. She told us, quite directly and in no uncertain terms, that speaking Spanish would "hold us back from being real Americans." She didn't want us to have a Mexican American accent, so we wouldn't suffer racism as she had. She wanted us to "pass" for white.

I have thought often about the pathology of my father's many addictions, and his inability to love his children. I have come to realize that his disease was the result of the intergenerational trauma of racism. He escaped the racism so prevalent in Arizona at the time to lose himself in the anonymity of the big city. My father escaped his reality in booze, drugs, women, and the horses. My father was a tortured man bent on escape.

My father could not love his children because he could not love himself, the person he was inside. Self-loathing is the stepchild of addiction. My dad felt unworthy of love because he felt so much hate from a racist society. And I have to believe he passed on those afflictions to my two brothers, as surely as he passed on his DNA, the color of their hair, their eyes, their smiles, and their sorrows.

My parents suffered for the sins of a racist society that made them want to be someone else other than the people they were born to be. I cannot blame them for wanting to pass as someone they were not. They were the victims of a viciously intolerable society. I can understand the fear that gripped people of color a generation ago. They simply wanted to live their lives and not be judged by the color of their skin. This is what America should be, and still is not, though some progress has been made.

Racism certainly has not disappeared in America. It is still as pervasive and insidious as ever, and the nasty voice of Nazism has grown louder in recent years. Still, I can see, within my own family and beyond, that more people are comfortable claiming their rightful heritage and honoring the blood that flows in their veins. My blood flows red. I have always identified as an indigenous man. And for this, I am proud.

It was my good fortune to come of age in the sixties, when it became acceptable, "cool," in fact, to be a Native American. I have lived in a time when it is acceptable to be the man I was born to be. Today, it is okay to be Navajo, Pima, or Mexican American, whomever I wish to claim in my heritage, whomever I feel most comfortable being. Whomever I am.

I cannot be angry that my parents never taught me Navajo, or Spanish. I learned Spanish on my own. It was my own responsibility to be the man whom I was born to be. I accepted my Mexican American heritage so I learned Spanish. I accepted also my Native American heritage, and this empowered me, enabled me, to work in a career that supported Native American projects.

It is an integral fact of my personal journey that I have always felt my Native heritage within me, though I was never exposed to it beyond my own efforts to connect. I recognize it is in my DNA. And, because I embraced my Native roots, because I was at peace with the person within, I was at peace with the world. More to the point, my personal journey has brought me to the place where I was able to do something positive and constructive, in my work with Friendship House, to help balance the scales of life and sobriety on the one side against the drug deaths of my brothers on the other side.

I know the Creator brought the Friendship House project to me so that I could help others like Sonny and Alex. I know that all my good work supporting Native projects is my way to honor my Native heritage and bring value to the community I was born to, though not born in. Balance and harmony are achieved in different ways. And sometimes, it takes years and many steps to arrive at restorative justice. I validate my contribution to Native values in the work I have done to help others, and I know my ancestors are looking at me and smiling.

Everything comes full circle. My parents rejected the heritage they were born to, out of the understandable fear of racism that controlled their lives. Today, I embrace the heritage I was born to, and I have, in my career, done what I can to support projects that uplift and uphold Native American values. It is a world of values whose time has come. The world has come full circle. The old wounds can heal. The scars may remain, but the pain is gone. *In beauty it is finished.*

San Francisco and Bill

AH, SAN FRANCISCO MEMORIES. I lived in San Francisco for most of my adult life. One thing I will always remember is the noise. Even at night. Especially at night.

The neighborhood where I owned a home was two blocks from a fire department. It was a crossroads busy as all hell. There were fire engines that ran down my street nonstop at every hour of the day and night. Must be a lot of false alarms in that town. The house was a mile from the juncture of two freeways, Interstate 101 and 280, down the hill from us. You could hear the constant insane din of nonstop freeway traffic, like a plague of cicadas. I heard that sound often in my dreams when I moved to Italy and for a long time after.

You would often hear gunshots, or maybe it was motorcycles backfiring. They seemed to happen a lot at night, so I imagined it was another bullet blasting from a pistol.

My nice but crazy neighbors next to me lived large and loved to party. They gathered on the front stoop of their house from about four in the afternoon till four in the morning. Drinking. A lot. By midnight there would be a lot of drunk people carousing. Then, they would engage in a contest to see who could throw their empty beer cans at the telephone pole across the street and hit the pole. Then, of course, there was the requisite celebration when someone scored a direct hit.

This was the fun part of the night. The fun soon segued rather suddenly and unpredictably into the violent-fist-fighting-women-screaming part of the night. These random acts of crazy occurred maybe three times a week and not necessarily only on the weekends.

I never understood how they could party so often. I only understood that I would never outlast them. They bought the house thirty years ago. They weren't going anywhere. I am gone, they remain there today, and so do the parties, I'm sure.

On my block, directly in front of my house, lived an angry single mom with a head full of fiery red hair who screamed at her poor kids all the time, inside the house and out. That seemed like the only way she could ever talk to them—screaming.

There was the teenage kid who had a loud race car with dual carburetors and no mufflers who liked to work on his car out front early on weekend mornings. I admired his early-to-rise approach to life, but it really interfered with my faint hopes for a quiet and peaceful cup of coffee on my front stoop at seven o'clock on a Sunday morning.

The local thoroughfare was a lively gentrified street with a bar with live music four nights a week. The best and most raucous bar was one block from me. In the wee hours, every weekend, carloads of people would cruise the street, having fun and playing loud music in their cars, windows wide open.

It would be easy to describe it as something like Mardi Gras on steroids turned vicious, but I've been to Mardi Gras twice, and Mardi Gras is really quite sedate by comparison and with much better music.

Every now and then in the adjacent yards behind my house the neighbors would set off fireworks. Cherry bombs and M-80s—that kind of thing. And not only on July 4.

But these issues I describe were relatively minor, though constant, aggravations to my peace of mind. You could call it the cost of living in a big city—the price one pays, like traffic jams, for having everything you could possibly want at any hour of the day or night. There was, however, one incident during my life in San Francisco that was more than an annoyance. It came close to being a matter of life and death.

It was during the time I was working on the Friendship House project, at a point in the project early on when I was focused on reaching out across various communities to forge supportive relationships and linkages with key constituencies. It was important to make alliances with nonprofits and community-based organizations outside of the Bay Area Native American community. We had to show that others were comfortable with the huge levels of financial backing that the city would have to dedicate to our project.

This activity required me to visit community-based, nonprofit organizations in all parts of the city, including those organizations based in the poorest parts of town, in the barrio and in the ghetto. I attended a lot of community town halls to make my case, not only to the decision-makers and gatekeepers of the community-based organizations but to the individual members of those communities. All of this work required me to speak at community meetings held in the evenings, when working people could attend. It was standard operating procedure for our effort, and I spent perhaps two years early on in the project enlisting this critical buy-in.

One evening, I drove into one of the toughest neighborhoods in San Francisco to give my talk about the Native American community and our plan to build this important residential treatment facility. The district was Bayview Hunters Point, and the meeting was in the local community center, in a dangerous place for an outsider after dark. I always wore a nice suit and tie to these meetings, my dress-for-success outfit that I felt was important for me to project an air of professionalism in representing my organization and community.

It was after dark when I arrived in the projects and drove around looking for the community hall where I was one of the scheduled speakers that evening. I drove around the unfamiliar surroundings, turning this way and that through the maze of side streets and byways that reminded me so much of the public housing projects where I grew up.

Everywhere I turned, my headlights would land on small groups of young men huddled together in conversation; they, in turn, would look up from whatever they were doing to stare at this unfamiliar vehicle cruising their territory. The faces were not welcoming, and I said a silent prayer that I would find my destination quickly, and in an area that was well lit.

I was fearful, no doubt about it. Many, many years before, when I first moved to San Francisco, I had found myself in another "bad" part of town, not really knowing the city that well yet. On that late afternoon long ago, as I was walking on the street looking for my friend's apartment, I turned a corner and found myself face to face with a gang—not just a bunch of guys, this was clearly a gang—of about two dozen young men and boys in their early teens about ten paces ahead of me. I looked in their faces, and they seemed to form a collective evil grin.

Then, without a word or any other cue among them, they all charged me, and I turned and ran as fast as I could. They caught up with me in no time. The guys in front tackled me, and then the rest is a blur. I started screaming for help, I was kicked, pummeled, I felt hands going through my pants pockets, and then someone hit me in the face with a bottle. The bottle broke across my left eye.

The chaos and pandemonium were over in an instant, though in that moment it seemed to go on forever. Certainly, too long. The kids whooped and hollered, as if making a victory cry on the battlefield, and then they took off running, turning the corner and disappearing down the streets of San Francisco, the city that I had always believed was all about love and peace and flower power.

A few residents in the neighborhood came out of their homes. Someone took me inside their house. Someone called an ambulance. I was bleeding profusely, and someone else picked the broken glass out of my face. They found my wallet on the ground, and it was largely intact except for the money that was gone. I had had five dollars in it. The ambulance arrived and took me to San Francisco General Hospital Emergency Room where they stitched me up and gave me antibiotics and pain meds.

The bottle had cut deeply into the skin around my eye, but, thank God, did not do any damage to my eyeball, nor did it impair my vision in any way. I still have the scar around my eye, and there was some reconstructive surgery that had to be done years later to remove the excess scar tissue that had formed over time as a result of the hastily completed sutures in the emergency room on that fateful summer afternoon.

But, fortunately, I had not sustained any other injuries other than a few bruises and aches, and I considered myself lucky to get off so easily. My guardian angel, once again, had done her job. It could have been much worse, I know. San Francisco perennially has one of the highest violent crime rates of any major city in the United States. Recent FBI data shows that violent crime in San Francisco is about 25 percent higher than in New York City, and about 50 percent higher than other major metropolitan cities in the country.

The mugging I suffered almost twenty years prior, and the city crime statistics of which I was well aware, were uppermost in my mind on that winter evening in the ghetto. My fears became even more intense once I parked and got out of my car. I had barely locked my car and moved away from it when a group of young men approached me, talking in low tones among themselves, too low for me to hear. I sensed that trouble was coming my way.

One of them said something to me about my nice suit, another one walked up to my car and asked if he could take a ride in it. I looked at them and tried to project an air of confidence, but my knees were shaking and I was at a complete loss of words. It was dark in that area, the nearby street lamp was broken. I had no idea where I was. My directions to the community hall were not very clear and it was nowhere to be seen. This was in the time before Google Maps and iPhones. I didn't know which way to go—if I should try to run, fumble my way back into my car, or try to be cool when inside I was screaming for salvation. I was sure they could smell my fear.

The small gang of eight or nine young men came nearer, the telltale swagger of danger in their steps. I thought I saw the flash of a knife in the hands of one of them close to me. I felt faint. I didn't think I could endure another such encounter in my life and get out alive again.

Then, one of the kids in the back of the group stepped forward and said something to me. I didn't understand what he said, but I looked at him. He walked up to me and said right in my face: "Hey, ain't you the guy who live next door to Devonte?" I looked at him and wasn't sure what the right answer should be.

It was true that Devonte was one of the kids in the house next to mine, the family that was in perpetual party mode. I didn't recognize this kid, but if he came over to visit Devonte often enough, then obviously he had seen me. It was my habit to sit on my front porch in the evening or on weekends, sipping a beer and watching the action on my street. "Yeah, that's me," I said, figuring I had nothing to lose at that point, trying to project an air of casual nonchalance.

"Hey y'all, he cool, les leave him be. I know this guy, he friends with Devonte." I looked from one face to another, trying to "read the room" in the dark. The dynamic changed almost immediately. They all loosened up with one motion of the pack. The guy in front put his knife away. The guy who recognized me smiled, and so did a couple of the others. The tension drained away like piss on dry ground. I felt like my bladder would go at any moment out of fear and relief.

"What you be doing here this time of night? Wanna buy something?" Devonte's friend asked me. "It's not safe for a guy like you," as he looked me up and down in my dress-for-success suit. I told him I was going to the meeting in the community hall. One of them said: "Oh, you be looking for that building way over there," and he pointed to it. "Come on, we can walk you to it. It ain't safe if you don't have protection." The guy who asked if he could take a ride in my car told me they would stay near my car to make sure no one would bother it.

Someone lit up a joint and offered it to me, but I politely declined. I was, after all, going to this public meeting to make a presentation on a drug treatment facility. Otherwise, I might have taken a hit merely to seal my bond with them, to show them I was cool, that I was just another kid like them from the hood.

When I got back from my presentation, which was a rousing success, my new friends were still hanging around my car, keeping it safe, protected. I told them I appreciated their help, and one of them said, it's okay, I was cool. As I drove my car out of those projects, a gentle mist just starting to drift down from the heavens, I thanked Devonte for being the kid next door, and I thanked my guardian angel for being right there with me once again.

It exhausts me to think of all the things that eventually turned me off to that lovely house that I once loved so much. My home for two years after retirement was in Italian olive country surrounded by three ancient stone villages just a few miles away. In Italy I could hear dogs barking at night, sometimes foxes or the occasional wolf howling. Even these sounds were sonorous, like the *lingua bella* of Italy, and it often sent me to sleep.

I love the quiet of Eureka, where I live. Maybe San Francisco was once like this. A city you could live in.

In the fall before I got sick with COVID, I returned to San Francisco for three months to help care for my friend Bill. Bill was suffering in the advanced stages of Crohn's disease, and he was in a bad way. I had come to San Francisco for a short, one-week visit in the final week of the baseball season just to watch the pennant race with Bill. One day, sitting in his yard over coffee one morning with another friend, Tom, Bill told us in no uncertain terms that he had been feeling real bad, and he did look bad.

He didn't ask for any help, but I saw how he was moving around, his pain was obvious, his movements slow and creaky. This was so unlike the energetic, always-up-for-anything, nonstop Bill, the guy who had long ago earned the nickname Sparky. I couldn't help myself. My heart poured out to him. Caught up in the moment, I said to Bill right then: "I'll move down here for a while and take care of you, Bill."

In less than a day, I found a room for rent in a nice house just one block from Bill, in the neighborhood I really loved and had lived in for many years when Bill and I were roommates with Alan long ago. I returned to Eureka to pack a bag for three months, then turned right around. It was the end of baseball season and the beginning of an autumn that I will always remember.

SAN FRANCISCO AND BILL

Bill and I would hang out all afternoon and into the evening. We'd watch football games, and at dinner I would buy us burritos at the taqueria. We talked about women and sports and all the great camping trips we had enjoyed together over the forty years we had been friends/brothers; and we watched his cat, Phillip, who would sit there staring at a blade of grass for an infinity.

Bill would start the day slowly, clearly in great pain, but as the day warmed up, so did Bill. It was wonderful when he got past the pain and became the Bill I've always known. When Bill is on, nothing can stop him. Sparky.

Between all the jokes and old stories retold again, we talked business: the business of Bill. I asked Bill for all the phone numbers I should have—his family, friends, doctor, hospital—anyone I needed to contact in an emergency. I asked him for the names of the prescriptions he was taking in case I needed to provide that information to a first responder. It wasn't a difficult conversation. It was done without comment or emotion. It was all business. The business of Bill.

I spent my first weeks there talking to local social service agencies that could be of some assistance to Bill long-term, after I was gone back home to Eureka. I spent time talking to Bill's other friends about the kind of support they might be able to provide if called upon. We created a phone tree of his support network. Bill is a great friend to all, and everyone was willing to do what they could to help this most true friend in need.

There was never any way I could tell Bill: *I will watch over you always.* But a few months were enough to know that we would always remember these beautiful days together. Just two brothers, hanging out, taking it one day at a time.

Nobody knows what the future will bring. We can only do what we can to be here with each other and for each other, ready for it, not knowing the "it" of it. The thing I did understand as I was caring for Bill is that I have seen too many dear people leave this world in recent years, and there was nothing I could do to help them or make things any easier for them or for the rest of us.

I knew I couldn't alter the course of Bill's destiny. That is not in anyone's hands. But I did know that I could affect his quality of life in this small way by being there with him. Bill and I have always been the closest of friends. It's not too much of him to ask me to help him change the channel on his remote, or pick up dinner for the two of us, or twist the cap off his bottle of juice. He had no strength for any of these simple things. The disease affected everything he did. I know he would do the same for me, and more, in a heartbeat. Of this, I am sure. Everyone tells me that what I'm doing "for Bill" is "so nice." But nice is not the word. The word is love. And I'm doing it as much for myself as I'm doing it for Bill.

Bill is my brother, the brother I never had, the surrogate for the brother who shoved me away from him when I was eight years old and who never wanted me to associate with him. Yes, Sonny did what he had to do for my own good, yes, I understand that now. Nevertheless, I wanted a big brother, I needed a big brother, and, at last, I had one in Bill.

Being there for Bill those three months felt like I had never really left San Francisco in the four years of back-and-forth between Italy and Eureka. When I was hanging out with Bill, the years of my travels and the lifetime of our friendship revealed in crystal clarity that I am blessed to be where I am today. Hanging out with Bill, having some laughs, making more great memories—this was all that mattered in the time that we shared in that endless autumn of our lives.

I will watch over you always, Bill. We are connected.

The Life of the Nomad

For as long as I can remember, I have been possessed of a fractured concept of home. It has always been easy for me to pull up stakes and move out and on, to another house, another city, across the country, or beyond. I have always been very comfortable in this mode; suitcase packed and at the ready, credit card in my pocket, passport in hand.

For as long as I can remember, I have loved to travel, to see the great natural and man-made wonders of the world, to discover what life is like for people in other cultures, to learn what lies beyond the horizon, beyond my field of vision. There is a thrill for me in finding myself in a strange new land, unfamiliar with the language, with people I do not recognize, and dependent on my own wits and common sense to get through every day. To adapt and to thrive.

And everywhere I have traveled, in all the unfamiliar places I have encountered, in all the times I have been surrounded by strangers in dark corners with no one at my back, I have never found myself in danger or regretted any path that I have ventured onto.

My guardian angel has been my constant, often sole companion on my adventures. Her words have been the refrain that plays background to the rhythm of the railroad tracks, or the tires humming on the highway, the din of jet engines singing in the stratosphere. Her words I took to heart, words I always believed, words that never seemed to fail me. *I will watch over you always.*

I can tell you the first time I felt this unshakeable wanderlust within my heart. It was the summer I flew off to college in the Bay Area from my home in Los Angeles. It was the first time I had ever been on a plane. I was very excited to be going to college, to be leaving Los Angeles, to be starting my life at last. All things were possible now, I knew.

As the jet took off from the runway, so did my spirit, lifting up off the tarmac in this remarkable machinery of flight surrounding me. My face was pasted to the window every minute of that short flight, as I picked out the contours of my home state below, familiar from all my geography lessons in school.

I was strapped into my seat, but nothing could contain my pure elation as the life that I had known was now dropping away, a blue, true dream of sky opening up before me. I still love to fly. Even now, a lifetime later, I thrill at the sensation of being upward bound, onward to some new adventure that lies ahead.

And I know my guardian angel loves to fly as well, staying close by me every mile of the way. In all my life's travels in the air, on the road, riding on trains or buses, I have never, ever had an accident or a delayed or cancelled flight, or missed a plane or a connecting flight or a train. I find this amazing. I have never been mugged in a foreign country, or robbed, or scammed in any way. I have had a remarkable run of good fortune wherever I have been in any of the twenty-four countries I have visited for pleasure or business. It has always been smooth sailing for me. I realize I have been blessed.

After I left my marriage to Carmen, I moved to Arizona to escape a past I was not happy with. I returned to Los Angeles after the pot incident, but I soon tired once again of Los Angeles and moved to the Shenandoah Valley of Virginia, where I lived for seven years and learned everything I could about organic gardening, another lifelong love of mine. After I completed college there, I went back to the West Coast to San Francisco, which had always been a favorite city since my high school memories of the summer of love.

Even though I have lived in San Francisco for most of my adult life, put down roots, bought a house, and with my wife raised a stepson, I never stopped traveling. I made regular major camping trips with my former roommates/brothers, Alan and Bill, or with my wife, flew to countries all over the world. These trips are too numerous to mention, but there remain more on my bucket list still.

And everywhere I have gone, I have always tried to stay in one place for as long as possible—Paris for three weeks, Barcelona for two weeks, Thailand for seven weeks (two times) to get the best sense of a place, to try to get to know the locals. I abhor the one-day, one-city mode of international travel. "If it's Tuesday, this must be Belgium," is the movie I never wanted to see. Quality, not quantity.

In my family, I am alone in my love for travel, in my wanderlust and nomadic spirit. My sister, whom I love dearly and with whom I've always shared a strong bond, cannot relate at all to me in this way. She lived in

Los Angeles, then with her husband moved to Eureka, bought a house, set down roots, and has been firmly planted here ever since. The extent of their traveling has been to L.A. to see family. One time, I took her with me to New York City as her birthday gift. Another time, she and her husband took up my offer to visit me in Italy for a month. I doubt she would ever have done these trips if not by my urging.

Certainly, no one else in my family "gets me." And I don't know anyone in my circle who has been so ready to hit the road at a moment's notice or move away out of state or out of the country. And herein lies the heart of the question "Why me?" that I have probed as deeply as I possibly can, not afraid to jam the stick into the hornets' nest.

I have come to believe in my darkest moments that it's not simply a matter of "some people like to travel," because I have known plenty of people who like to travel. For me, there is something that goes deeper than an interest in adventure. For me, it is my comfort, my control, my escape, my pathology, even. I believe it goes back, all the way back to the day I was born, to this *fractured concept of home.* I believe that when my mom abandoned me, forcing me to fend for myself, to make do without the normal, healthy, natural sense of security and comfort of maternal love, she unwittingly created in me a nascent sense that I could not rely on anyone else, that I was on my own in life. From birth, the lesson I believe I learned was how to fend for myself, that I could not trust anyone but myself.

Because if you can't trust your mother, who can you trust? Who should you trust? Where is your home, if it's not with your parents? The answers all came up the same—me, and me alone.

And when Mom took me back at six months, the lessons she imparted to me were mostly negative messages of weakness, of stupidity, of rejection. It was when I was out of her reach, beyond her negative expectations for me, and in a classroom all day with encouragement and support, that I began to blossom, to show just who I was and could be, to prove that I had value. Out in the world, I could survive, I could flourish. At home, I was stifled, undervalued, unwanted.

Another aspect of my fractured concept of home was the realization in my young life in the projects of East Los Angeles that there had to be a better world, a better place than the one I was in right now.

My first cogent, coherent thought I can ever recall was of a time I was sitting on the curb outside our unit in the projects, on Hunter Street, staring at the black asphalt of the street, rubbing the burning smog out of my eyes, my little chest hurting from the toxic fumes of cars rolling by. I looked around at what I instinctively, intuitively understood was an ugly sight all around me, and I do clearly remember saying to myself: "There has to be a better place than this."

How does a child of five years old understand such a thing, when he knows of nothing else in life? Perhaps in the same way that my brother understood that it was too late for him, that his path in life was already determined.

My lifelong wanderlust, my search for a better world, a better life, has its genesis in that little boy's primordial, life-affirming question to himself, before that little boy even dared to speak words to anyone else. It may have appeared to others that I was a deaf-mute or stupid, as my mother believed, but I was fully aware, thinking deeply, and merely keeping my powder dry.

A good deal of research in recent decades by developmental psychologists has shown that resilient children in at-risk environments have what psychologists call an "internal locus of control," meaning that they believe from the earliest age that they can determine their own fates. These children are able to manage the world on their terms, are independent thinkers, learn quickly how to stand on their own two feet, and learn to use their natural skills effectively in the face of very difficult circumstances. Resilience has less to do with certain innate psychological traits. It is more about the ability to adapt to a given situation. Child resilience theory has helped me understand a lot about myself and my development throughout the years, and how I have turned much adversity to my advantage. It has even helped to explain a lot about my career path.

I flourished in a long professional career as a strategic planner for nonprofit organizations. My work has always involved looking at the landscape of threats, opportunities, strengths, and weaknesses that organizations face and helping them develop the programs and plans that can enable them to flourish in constantly shifting and challenging environments. In my own life, I have always tried to consider the worst possible scenario of any choice or situation and work the options back from there to choose a path to success. "What's the worst that can happen here?" I ask myself. "And, what can I do about it?" It seems my whole life has been geared toward fixing my sights on the route that gets me beyond the trouble, leaving little to chance.

When I think about my brother, Sonny, I see a very different personality and approach to life. Where I may have been risk averse, or trying to minimize risk, Sonny from the earliest age seemed bent on taking huge risks. At the age of five, Sonny got hit by a car crossing the street at the wrong place. He ended up in the hospital with a broken leg and other broken bones. In grammar school, he tried to jump over a volleyball net, on a dare, and got his foot caught in it and crashed his head on the asphalt schoolyard—another trip to the hospital. Playing baseball, he took a wild and risky chance to steal second base and crashed into a plateglass window, and he was back at the hospital.

There are many other events like these too numerous to mention that speak to Sonny's constant tendency to make the wrong move at his peril. I'm sure every family has their own Sonny—the kid who always ended up in the hospital.

I, on the other hand, never broke a bone, never got hurt, never went to the hospital because of foolish behavior, always was too careful not to do anything that might hurt me. Rather than roughhouse with Sonny and the other boys in the neighborhood, I chose to stay inside with my little sister, Jo Ann, and play dolls with her. I remember Sonny always trying to coax me to join them in a game of football outside, and I always refusing, staying inside with Jo Ann. My mom told me years later that she actually thought I was gay because I preferred to play with dolls with Jo Ann and not normal boy stuff. I remember that I enjoyed my sister's company more and chose the more tranquil way to spend a Saturday afternoon. Not gay, just risk averse. I never got hurt playing dolls, and that suited me just fine.

But risk-averse behavior, or child resiliency theory, can go only so far in explaining the events in our lives or the choices we make. I may have consciously or subconsciously tried to deal with my environment in the best way, the safest way, but there are many other factors beyond our control that influence our lives. I have said before that my mother's subtle and blatant abuse continued in various ways throughout my childhood. I have said that I always felt I had to be perfect, bring home straight As to be accepted. But I could never do enough, nor could I ever be enough to please her.

When I was a senior in high school, my mother caved in to the stresses in her life over Sonny, Raul, money, and more. When I started dating Carmen in high school and staying out late, like a typical teenager, the perfect little student no more, my mother began to crack.

Although I still was making grades good enough to earn a full scholarship to the college of my choice, my mother began to go unhinged, because she thought that I was going bad. I never drank, I never smoked, I never did drugs, I never ditched school. I still got good grades. I had a girlfriend, that was all; but to Mom, that signaled the end of the son she could no longer control. If I wasn't perfect, I wasn't worthy.

One Saturday afternoon in April, two months before my graduation, I went to Carmen's in defiance of my mother's orders. When I got back later that day, all my clothes and books had been thrown out of my bedroom window, and she had locked me out of the house. She yelled at me through the back door that if I wanted to be with Carmen all the time, I should move in with her. I was no longer welcome in her house.

I gathered up my things, threw them in my car, and drove to Carmen's house to tell her what had happened. When I got there, Carmen told me that my mother had called with a message for me to call her, and I thought she was going to tell me to come home, that she had overreacted.

I called Mom, and she told me that if I didn't bring the car back immediately she would report it as stolen and I would be arrested. She even had the name and badge number of the cop she had talked to at the police station as proof of her intentions. The car was, of course, registered in her name. I knew my mother. I had no doubt she would have me arrested as she promised. I drove back to my (no longer) home, with Carmen and her parents following me, parked the car in the driveway, and left the keys on the hood.

As I was driving back to the home that was no longer mine in the darkening evening sky of early April, I turned on the radio to my local rock station. The Beatles song "Blackbird" came on the air. The *White Album* had been released the year before, and I, and everyone I knew, had bought it immediately and played it all the time. I knew every song from beginning to end.

Now, the lyrics to "Blackbird" resonated within me with a force that felt prophetic. I could not help but believe that the words were directed at me, telling me that I had only been waiting all my life for this moment to be free. Today, whenever I hear this song, I am transported in time to that evening and to the feeling I had then—that this was now the true beginning of my life, my road to freedom. That no matter what I faced from this day forward, I had to face it alone. I could never count on anyone. I could count on only myself. And I was free. Free of all the baggage that held me back. Free to be my own person. The architect of my own destiny. The master of my own destiny. Resilient. Always maintaining the locus of control.

Staying in Carmen's house was out of the question. Her parents were strict Catholic Cubans, not open-minded types at all. They made this clear to me from the outset, so I had only one option. I became homeless, before the modern term came into the vernacular. Carmen gave me some blankets and a pillow, hid my clothes in her closet, and for the next five months, until I flew off to college and dormitory life, I slept on the grass in a nearby park, or, when it rained now and then, I scaled the fence of an auto junkyard and slept in the back seat of the largest car I could find. Carmen brought me food in the mornings, and her parents were kind enough to feed me every evening.

Carmen's parents never asked nor wanted to know where I was sleeping. I'm sure they believed that I or my mother would soon relent. For a mother to treat her son like this was incomprehensible to them, they often admitted to me.

She never threw Sonny out of the house despite the fact that his behavior was far more egregious, far more dangerous, if you want to compare bad behaviors. She seemed to have an endless reservoir of patience for his repeated transgressions, not only of her "orders" but of the law.

This unfair, unequal treatment served as a reminder that her fuse with me had always been intolerably short. She never cut me any slack. I could not help thinking, as I rocked myself to sleep on the back seat of a filthy junkyard car, that she had never wanted me anyway, and she had finally gotten what she wanted—to have me out of her life.

It was a horrible life that spring and summer, and often scary, and I cried a lot on those eternally long nights under such squalid conditions. I went to school every day, washing up in the boys' room, doing my homework in the school library. When I graduated in June, no one in my family attended the ceremony. Mom never reached out to me, nor did I break down and call her. I figured if she was fine with the way things were now, then I should just move on and adjust. There is sad irony in my mom's extreme overreaction to my relationship with Carmen that is not lost on me. Instead of reining me in and forcing me to change my behavior, it had, of course, the opposite effect—the law of unintended consequences.

My mother kicked me out of the house two months before my high school graduation, then I would be off to college in the San Francisco Bay Area four hundred miles away. It's very likely that my eighteen-month high school romance with Carmen would have ended at that point, and perhaps I would have met someone else or buried myself in my books and moved on to a new and different life.

What my mother's actions did, in fact, were to keep me in Carmen's orbit, in her arms, and they forced me to stay close to her and her family.

For now, Carmen's family became my refuge. Nearly four years would pass before my mother and I would reconnect. To this day, I still cannot recall how the impasse broke. Suffice it to say, the scars from that wound remain, try as I might to forgive and forget.

I can tell you that the rupture that began at birth became permanent and unrelenting. She and I have nothing resembling a good relationship even now. We never fight, we never argue, we just barely engage with each other and only on the most superficial levels. Weeks will go by between phone calls, and though she lives less than two miles from me, I hardly ever go to visit her. I suppose that's on me, but I feel no love for her.

It sounds harsh, I know, but it's the unvarnished truth. There is no point in lying or sugarcoating the thing we have, or don't have. It is what it is. I had to long ago come to terms with how she feels about me, and the only way I know how to respond is in kind.

There has been other long-term residual or collateral damage to me as a result of my inability to bond with my mother. I have demonstrated throughout my life a consistent pattern of failing to tolerate serious breaks in trust in the love relationships I have experienced. I can be a faithful and loving partner, a supportive man, a constant compromiser, and I can accept human frailties or mistakes of many kinds in love. I have many close, lifelong friends, men and women, and I can be very loyal and accepting in these relationships.

But when it comes to serious, committed loving relationships, I have always drawn a firm line at infidelity or, in a similar situation, where my lover has committed a fundamental breach of trust. I have walked out on several significant long-term loves, including marriage, where there was infidelity, or trust has been betrayed and I have been stabbed in the back.

If I have been done wrong by a cheating partner, I don't bother sticking around to give her a chance to do it again. There is no turning back for me. This was the reason I left Carmen. I could not accept that she had cheated on me so soon after we got married and after I had sacrificed my lifelong dream of college. This has been my guiding philosophy in love. It may be a good or bad trait, but it is what it is, and that is my Achilles' heel.

Today, I can understand my mother's fears and anxieties at the time. Sonny was on his way to a life of prison. When I started to rebel and stand up to her in my own harmless way—dating a girl in high school—she thought that I, too, was "turning bad." I suppose she felt that she needed to quickly put the lid on my emerging rebellion, or she would lose me, like she lost Sonny.

What she never understood was that she had lost me a long time ago, at my birth, when she had told them in the hospital to take me away. I suppose she thought she was teaching me a lesson by throwing me out of the house, but the lesson I learned was the wrong one. To me, it was merely another episode in a life of abusive behavior. I saw her treatment of me as just another form of rejection. I don't think that is so far fetched for a sensitive kid of seventeen to presume.

Sadly, her reaction backfired for both of us. In the short term, it would set me on a dangerous downward spiral that I would not be able to pull myself out of for at least five years, culminating in that low point that could easily have resulted in self-fulfilling my mom's worst fears of seeing me go into the criminal justice system like Sonny.

That seminal trigger event, smuggling pot across the border, required serious intervention by my guardian angel to save me from that worst possible outcome. In the long term, it would permanently affect my relationship to my mother and to the other significant love relationships I have had in my life.

My poor mother, bad luck followed her like a shadow. Bad decisions recoiled on her like the kick of a shotgun, ricocheting straight back into her heart. Penury of the spirit, destitution of the soul were her constant companions. I see that now, but back then, a sensitive and uncertain seventeen-year-old, I could do nothing for her, struggling to find my own way in a world that had turned suddenly harsh and brutally cold.

I will watch over you always. Even when you have been abandoned by those you should be able to trust. So the fracture in my concept of home, the reason I never felt bound to any one particular place, this nomadic spirit that I have enjoyed as a world traveler open to change and a new life has as much to do with pain as with joy.

I have come to see that I learned from my first moments in life to adapt quickly to any sudden change in my world: adapt or perish. Move as fast as you can away from trouble, and survive. Traveling is a good and wonderful thing, and I have enjoyed it immensely for all the right reasons. But deep within, the roots of my wanderlust lie dark and tangled. Like most things in life, it is an interplay of light and dark, good and bad, coexisting in both joy and sorrow, and it is up to us to find the balance that keeps us moving in the right direction.

I take comfort from the words in that image on my mother's bedroom wall in the projects. *I will watch over you always.* These words have been my constant companions, when I had no other thoughts to comfort me, when I had no one else to turn to. On occasion, I find myself singing the words to "Where Is Love," by Lionel Bart, from the musical *Oliver*. And the burning question at the heart of this song: "Does it fall from skies above?" This song always brings a tear to my eye.

> *If I speak in the tongues of mortals and of angels, but do not have love, I am a noisy gong or a clanging cymbal.*
>
> *And if I have prophetic powers, and understand all mysteries and all knowledge, and if I have all faith, so as to remove mountains, but do not have love, I am nothing.*
>
> *If I give away all my possessions, and if I hand over my body so that I may boast, but do not have love, I gain nothing. (1 Cor 13:1–3)*

Another Close Call

As we get older, those pesky floaters in our eyes, those little spots, flecks, or strings that drift across our field of vision, they come and go, and they can be very annoying. Most of the time, they are only annoying. But sometimes, they can be a symptom of serious damage taking place in real time, an actual medical emergency that requires immediate attention.

Most floaters are caused by normal, age-related changes that indicate the vitreous substance inside our eyeballs is drying up. Getting old is all about drying up, losing muscle mass, hair falling out, vision fading. All well and good and fine but not always harmless, as I was to discover one day.

These normal-seeming floaters were persisting in my eye for a few days, and I was figuring I should probably have them checked out. This was in the time before Google internet searches, and getting instant and easy access to information about every subject under the sun was not possible. We all relied on sharing medical or health info among our friends, a real "old people's" habit, turning into our parents, as we were all beginning to realize, talking all the time about our aches and pains, boring anyone younger than forty-five years of age.

Every one of my friends whom I had asked about floaters all said the same thing. Yes, they were annoying. But no one knew or said anything about the real potential for problems with them. So, in my annual eye exam one year, I talked to my ophthalmologist about them when I entered the exam room. He looked into my eyes with his equipment, and after a few minutes and several pieces of equipment later, he told me he needed to refer me to the folks over at laser surgery at Kaiser.

I pulled out my pocket calendar so we could discuss the date and time to schedule this procedure, and he said to me: "Oh no, I've got to get you in there right away. You're not going anywhere." I was a bit stunned.

He then explained to me what he was seeing. He said that the retina was detaching from my right eye. If that happens, I would go blind in that eye, and, once that happened, there was nothing they could do to restore my vision. He said it could happen in a week, or a day, or in a few hours; it was that bad, that far advanced. I just stared at him.

I was now more than stunned. I was in a state of shock. I sat there while he called the laser department and set me up for the procedure within the hour. He gave me directions and sent me on my way across the street and up the block. His last words to me as I left his office were: "Don't walk too fast or move your head too quickly, or you could dislodge the retina." I started praying real hard. I began to feel like I would cry. I wondered if the tears would be a problem for my eye. The laser surgery proceeded without a hitch. It consisted of a laser cauterizing the retina, basically "welding" it to the back of the inside of the eyeball in the places it had torn away. There were four or five of these "spot welds" they had to do. But the procedure was completed in less than an hour and went according to plan.

My eye was now repaired. The surgeon told me I was lucky to come in when I did. He confirmed the frightening diagnosis that the ophthalmologist had delivered to me earlier. I thanked my lucky stars. I thanked my guardian angel. I had dodged a bullet to my eyeball and had been completely oblivious to imminent threat. I felt again the watchful eyes of my guardian angel, making sure my eyes would get the attention they needed in the nick of time.

You don't get an owner's manual of routine maintenance or things to watch for in health matters. And so many little aches and pains and annoying twitches or deviations from the norm can end up being much more than annoying or little. Excessive scratching can be a very early symptom of a dangerous form of leukemia, to illustrate just one small example.

When I first got sick with COVID, I didn't expect it to metastasize into the near-fatal form that it eventually took. My fever came and went, some days were good and some were bad, it seemed for a while like just the flu. This was at a time when they were telling people not to go to the emergency room for "every little ache and pain." It was winter, after all, and it could be the flu or the common cold, which it resembled.

So I brushed off the worst of it and thought it was over on the days I felt okay. I wonder now how things may have gone badly for me had I not gone to the hospital when I did. It's true that my guardian angel is always watching out for me, but I also keep in mind the other saying that I heard as I was growing up: "God helps those who help themselves."

It is important to have faith that a benevolent deity cares for us, but we also must have agency in our lives and take initiative at the right time. I pray for the common sense to know the difference between faith and self-realization, the fulfillment by oneself of the possibilities open to us.

Life to me seems like a great circle. And in every moment, in every day, we stand at the center of that great circle. The path we walk through life takes us out along a radius to the circumference of the great circle of life. We have an entire 360 degrees of choices in the direction we take along our radius, as we walk outward toward the great, ever-expanding circle of life. Ultimately, we will end up on the circumference.

But where we end up on the circumference of that circle depends very much on the direction we started out from. If we had taken one small step differently, if we had turned just one degree in this way or that as we stood at the center of our circle of life, our path along the radius would have taken us to a much different place on the circumference, at the end of our great journey in this ever-expanding circle of life. Even one small step different, one little move this way or that, and things end up very differently way out on that circumference.

Sometimes, the smallest choices or the seemingly inconsequential decisions we make may not seem like such a big deal at the time. But out there, along the circumference, a degree or two, one step this way or that way back at the center can end up taking us to a very different point, far from the point where we might have originally ended up.

The circle of life is an amazing metaphor that we hear about all the time. That metaphor has come to make a lot more sense to me the older I get and the more I see how little decisions along the way can often make all the difference in the world, at the outer edge of the ever-expanding circle of life.

Anthony Bourdain and the Art of Travel

Anthony Bourdain is one of my revered heroes of contemporary America. Bourdain was everything I would like to be: master chef, delightful raconteur, prolific writer, inveterate world traveler, and engaging personality. The thing I admired most about the man was that he pulled himself out of a serious drug habit and turned his life around before it was too late, giving us some of the best years of his life after he beat his drug addiction.

It broke my heart when Bourdain committed suicide. It felt like I had lost a close personal friend. I was despondent for days. I could not understand why he had taken his own life at the peak of his career. I still don't understand, but I have stopped trying to, choosing instead to take what joy I can from the words and wisdom he left to us.

People the world over love their food, their drink, their music; and most of all, they love to share these simple pleasures with family, with friends, and with any stranger who appreciates and respects their food and their hospitality. These are the things we all have in common—the incontrovertible bonds of our humanity, as basic as bread, as right as laughter, as true as a teardrop. Language, culture, religion, politics, and borders may separate us, tribalize us, pit one person—one nation—against the other; but if we sit together over a meal, those differences melt away, and a little space is created in which we see how much we really are alike beneath the surface, no matter where we come from.

Anthony Bourdain understood this more than most. He felt these basic truths keenly, beyond mere comprehension. It was, in fact, his life credo—a core value of his, which, my intuition tells me, may have pushed him to the farthest edge of despair as he sat alone in his hotel room in France that June day in 2018 when he took his own life.

I have been an avid fan of Bourdain since 2001, when my friend/brother Bill gave me a copy of Bourdain's *Kitchen Confidential* for my birthday. I will go even further and admit that I have been, in fact, a fawning, adoring, unabashed devotee of the man, and I will be forever grateful to Bill for having brought me into the world of Anthony Bourdain.

Bourdain exploded into the limelight with his groundbreaking, truth-telling *Kitchen Confidential*, taking readers behind the scenes and sharing with us the dark and dirty secrets of high-end restaurant kitchens and the people who make them work. His cocky, achingly funny, brash, and drug-fueled take-no-prisoners attitude heralded the dynamic arrival of a vibrant young rebel in the culinary and literary world. He inflamed the interest of a nation of diners from the get-go. He had me hooked from page 1.

But the man wasn't just about restaurant reviews or new foodie trends or the vicious "who is in and who is out" in the culinary kingdom. Bourdain soon evolved, as his fame grew quickly and as he explored ever-widening platforms for his heartfelt beliefs about the value of good food, a quality dining experience, and how the two come together and are expressed in and through culture.

Following on the heels of his overnight success with *Kitchen Confidential*, Bourdain two years later developed *A Cook's Tour*, his first food and world travel television show, and, soon after, hosted a new program along the same lines blending culinary and cultural adventure with *No Reservations*.

The premiere in 2013 of *Parts Unknown* manifested the full flowering of Bourdain's enormous talent, insights, and profound appreciation for cuisines and cultures until his death five years later. His first book created a new paradigm for culinary literature. His ventures into television also broke the mold for both food and travel shows. Bourdain's focus was less about natural wonders or man-made masterpieces than about people, their lives, their hopes, their concerns.

What is revealed in his programs, especially throughout the 104 episodes of *Parts Unknown*, is that Bourdain was more than a master chef and world traveler. He was an agnostic humanist by the classic definition of the term. He believed in the value and goodness of all human beings and in our common human needs. He did not believe in a higher power that guides our lives and behavior, believing instead that human experience provides the only moral code to live by.

This is a well-documented fact. Bourdain was outspoken about his views on god and religion. For him, sharing a meal with a stranger, or someone who holds radically different views from yours, is the true path to enlightenment.

A big part of Bourdain's personal appeal was his honesty, sincerity, genuineness. His willingness to open himself to the audience without pretense that came through in *Kitchen Confidential* became his abiding ethos on television. He never held back in front of the camera, and the result was that we knew we were watching a real man confronting real truths in real time. It was a quality that endeared him to his audience.

Bill knew that I would relate to Bourdain on all the most important ways that mattered. I love to cook for myself and for my friends, and I love to explore new ways to make a good meal better.

I also share Bourdain's love for travel, near and far—anywhere, anytime, any way. For me, travel is a lifelong passion that goes back to that little boy growing up in the projects, when my first lucid and vivid memory was that "there has to be a better place than this." As I got older and learned just how much bigger and more beautiful the world is, I set out on the road and never looked back. I have been traveling ever since.

In my twenties, I set out first to discover America, driving back and forth across the country from coast to coast. I lived for years in different parts of the country, getting to know what life was like for people in the Southwest, in the Deep South, in New England. In my thirties, I began to explore the rest of the world, beginning with Mexico and Canada, then traveling the many diverse countries of Europe. In the next decade, my insatiable passion for the road took me to Asia and South America.

By that point in my life I was fortunate to have been able to establish my own business at home that gave me a lot of independence and flexibility in my schedule, and I now had the resources and the time to vacation for two to three months a year. I returned for extended stays to many of the places I had discovered in my earlier adventures and found many other new places to explore.

But the things that make me feel such affinity for Bourdain, that make me feel we were kindred spirits, go beyond the simple passions for food and travel. I learned a fundamental lesson on my journeys in life and in the world that Bourdain lived and articulated and manifested better than I could ever hope to.

Early on, I learned the simple and invaluable truth that if you show you appreciate the food your hosts love, they will accept you with open arms. I never turned up my nose at the local specialty of the house, and I have never regretted it.

And through this openness to and from others, I learned another important lesson Bourdain understood: that no matter where you go, anywhere in the world, we are all the same. We all enjoy the same simple, irreducible human pleasures: the comfort food we grew up with, our local brew, the songs that define us, our community that supports us.

The unique appeal of *Parts Unknown* was that Bourdain chose to break bread with real folk, on their terms, in their homes and on their backstreets. He was not about haute cuisine. He was about the soul food of foreign lands, in the slums, off the food carts, in the jungles even.

Anywhere people were eating, Bourdain was there, standing in someone's back yard, or squatting on a tiny stool in an open-air market, or sitting cross-legged on the ground in the savannah. He never shied away from drinking whatever the locals offered.

Sure, Bourdain took us with him to the great capitals of the world and dined with celebrities in the finer establishments. But he also charted new territory as a travel host by getting far off the beaten path and eating at places that would never appear in TripAdvisor. And as savvy and comfortable as he was in Paris, or New York, or Tokyo, he was, above all, a humble man who understood deeply just how lucky he was to be in his position.

In *Parts Unknown*, we see a man who seeks out and shares home-cooked meals and deep conversations with people who live at the very edges of survival—the poor, the uncounted, the unseen. As open as he was to their food, Bourdain was also wide open to the people he met, in all their myriad quirks of humanity.

Bourdain was nonjudgmental about people and their food. This was a central tenet of his personality, his worldview. In an interview not long before he died, Bourdain recalled what Mark Twain wrote: "Travel is fatal to prejudice, bigotry, and narrow-mindedness." I would take that one step further, and say that travel endears you to humankind everywhere. I am sure this is how Bourdain felt.

Bourdain had a true gift for showing us what most travelers rarely see—or care to see. How real people live who have to struggle just to feed their families, people who never had the luxury of travel beyond their small patch of the world. And when he was with those who had so very little, he was moved by their generosity to share what little they had, and the joy they had for the intangible richness of their lives, like family. His recurring theme is the unconditional giving nature of those who have so little, by our materialistic standards.

This is not to say that he dwelled on the sadness in people's lives or sought out cheap moments of television pathos for the sake of ratings. Everywhere Bourdain went, people opened up to him, sharing their joys as well as their concerns. But because Bourdain did not shrink from visiting the troubled spots in the world, places like Myanmar, Gaza, the Congo, Iran, Manila—where repressive governments held sway, or chaos and conflict ruled, or child mortality and poverty rates were high—his transparent honesty before the camera exposes much about his sensitive nature and the depth of his compassion for others.

If we pay attention to Bourdain as he listens to others and draws them out about their lives, their dreams and their problems, if we pause the image for a moment and study Bourdain's face, we can see in his eyes an empathy for the oppressed and, I believe, a sense of shared pain in what they endure.

Nowhere is this more evident than in the first episode of season 7 of *Parts Unknown* when Bourdain visits Manila at Christmastime. We join Bourdain as he meets rock musicians in a biker bar, tours the city eating street food, and spends a wild evening at a company Christmas party eating *lechon* (roast pork) by the handful, playing drinking games and musical chairs. The episode ends in the home of a Filipino family sharing their Christmas meal with Bourdain.

As he talks with the family about their lives and the ways they have coped with the poverty that is their lot in life, the telling close-ups of Bourdain reveal in his eyes powerful moments of genuine understanding on his part, of unscripted empathy. We see how the family is clearly full of love for each other and happy to be together at the holidays, and one can't help but feel the unnerving sense in Bourdain of something he feels he is missing in his life.

The scene is a poignant, heartrending moment of vulnerability. For all the success, freedom, and recognition Bourdain has enjoyed, it seems to me in this episode that something may be missing that he cannot find in his travels.

While the world was truly Bourdain's community, and he certainly knew how to make friends and was genuinely loved like family wherever he went, I have to stop and wonder how deeply Bourdain was affected by that particular traveler's remorse that finds you in some foreign land at Christmastime, far from your own hearth and home. I have often tried to understand what lies at the core of my own passion for being on the road again. There have been times I have asked myself: what am I looking for, or what am I trying to escape?

Was Bourdain in search of something in his travels that he could not find? Was he trying to make some connection to the world among strangers that did not exist closer to home? Anthony Bourdain offered us his unique perspective on the world. He shared with us a vision of the world of food and travel that never existed before him. But what was it that he saw that he could not share?

We don't know what he felt at the end. His schedule was brutal. His work took him on the road 260 days a year, and he had an eleven-year-old daughter back home. His friend Eric Ripert, who was filming with him in France in those final days, said that Bourdain had been in a state of exhaustion.

Bourdain spoke honestly and forthrightly about his drug addiction. This is another reason I feel a kinship, a brotherly love for Bourdain. Not a day goes by that I don't think about my brothers, and it's been decades since they overdosed. Now, I find myself thinking also of Bourdain every day. I still mourn the man. I still grieve our loss.

We who have this insatiable wanderlust within come to see, at some point, especially as we get older, that halfway around the world we are sacrificing precious time that we are not spending with our friends and families back home. As a perennial "stranger in a strange land," I have seen my new friends go home at the end of the evening while I return alone to my hotel room.

I realize it is vanity to think that I may have some clue as to what pushed Bourdain too hard on his last day. No one can say what led him to such a dark place. I certainly don't pretend to. I can only interpret what I understand from his words based on my own experiences, biases, and failings.

But I do know beyond any doubt that Bourdain was a man who lived life fully, felt compassion deeply, and experienced an understanding of people by opening up his own heart—relentlessly and without filters—to their lives. I wonder if he may have suffered too much on their behalf, carrying their burdens deep within—if, in a sense, he felt and loved too much.

Bourdain wrote an essay in 2010 called "My Aim Is True," in which he profiles the work of Justo Thomas, a middle-aged Dominican who works in the kitchen at New York's Le Bernardin restaurant. Thomas's sole job six days a week is to break down and carve up the more than seven hundred pounds of fresh fish the restaurant will serve to its customers that day.

In almost seven years working there, Bourdain tells us, Thomas has never eaten in the dining room of Le Bernardin. He can't afford it. Bourdain remarks to Thomas that some of the patrons are ordering a bottle of wine that costs as much as Thomas makes in two months. To which Thomas replies: "I think in life they give too much to some people and nothing to everybody else."

We will never know, of course, but I wonder if Bourdain could not reconcile himself to the vast and severe inequality that exists among the rich and the poor, the huge disparity among those that have and those that have not, and among those who travel the world in search of something they come to realize may never satisfy some unknowable, unforgiving emptiness inside.

In discovering Bourdain's life, I have come to feel that I understand something important about the man. More to the point, I know that I have come to understand something about myself and my own particular wanderlust, my enjoyment of fine cuisine and street food, and my relentless need to express myself in the written word.

That "something" I have come to realize finally, is that my home is here, in my heart, and in this place where I am now and where I will stay—a pleasant little spot in Northern California. It is a place that has everything a man could possibly want in life—a loving family, some very good restaurants, and lots of taped episodes of *Parts Unknown*.

I never tire of watching these episodes over and over again. And every time I do, I feel I have lost a dear friend in Anthony Bourdain, a friend who has helped me to find myself at long last. I feel that Bourdain will be with me always, and watching over me in my travels.

And someday, I will hit the road again, when this plague of COVID has been spent, and the first place I will travel to is this land where I was born, to see the sights I have always loved in the Great American West.

I will return to the Range of Light, to the great Sierras of California, to this place that is the dawn of dreams, and to the other great open spaces of America.

Nothing else other than love has ever made me feel so alive, to be standing in the presence of such natural beauty. Yosemite. Grand Canyon. Oak Creek Canyon. Cochise Stronghold. Zion. Death Valley. Shenandoah National Park. Wupatki. Chaco Canyon. Big Bend. Volcanoes National

Park. The Everglades. Acadia. Capitol Reef. Mount Rainier. Mono Lake. Aransas National Wildlife Refuge. Pinnacles National Monument. The Carrizo Plain. Saguaro. Cape Cod. Cape Hatteras. The Great Smoky Mountains. The Great Basin. Joshua Tree. Mesa Verde. Lassen. Lake Tahoe. Haleakala. Rocky Mountain National Park. Bandolier. Redwood National Park. Canyonlands. Bryce. Mount Shasta. Big Sur.

I love our national parks and any open spaces where nature can breathe freely. So many trips I have done. So many more still to do. And someday, I will return to my dreams. And always, I know my guardian angel will be there with me, whispering in my ear: *I will watch over you always.*

Near-Disaster in the High Sierra

BILL PLANNED A MAJOR backpacking trip into the High Sierra one summer and invited me to join him and his family. Coming on the trip were his brother Danny and Danny's son, Eric; Bill's cousin Fred and Fred's son (I forget his name); and another friend, Don. I asked my twelve-year-old stepson if he would like to join us, and he eagerly agreed.

We were hiring packhorses and a guide to haul our gear to a predetermined site near a high mountain stream, in a place called the Minarets. Bill was going to ride a horse because he had recently broken his arm. The rest of us would carry daypacks and hike the seven miles one way along an occasionally visible but unmarked trail. Bill and Danny had done this trip years ago, and we were going with the same outfitter.

I didn't think to bring my own map. That was my first mistake. Trusting Bill's brother, Danny, to get us there safely was my second mistake.

The day started beautiful and warm and perfect and stayed that way throughout our ordeal. This was a small miracle, indeed, as the High Sierra in that time of the summer could often whip up unexpected lightning storms without warning. I did worry about that possibility, but as we got underway from San Francisco in the predawn hours, it did not seem like the weather would pose any risk for the next few days.

We all arrived in separate cars around the same time at the pack station early in the morning. Our gear was loaded onto the mules, and Bill was given some basic horse riding lessons. The rest of us filled our water cans, ate a light meal of fuel food, checked our packs for enough water and peanut-butter-and-jelly sandwiches and granola bars, and set off on a clear and visible hiking trail, starting off at an elevation of around 8,000 feet toward our makeshift campsite at 11,000 feet.

Bill and the guides and packhorses took the horse trail. We were taking plenty of provisions in the horse packs, and we hoped to catch some nice fat rainbow trout in the stream where our campsite was situated.

NEAR-DISASTER IN THE HIGH SIERRA

We figured we would do the seven miles in about five hours. We figured wrong.

Things went well for the first couple of hours. We were all in high spirits, and Danny kept telling me how well he knew the trail since he and his family had done this hike years ago. So I assumed he knew the trail, and I also assumed he had a good map, in case he may have forgotten some things here and there. Note to Ray: Always carry your own map. P.S.: Never again trust Danny. At some point around the middle of the day, the trail disappeared. Just vanished without a trace.

We did know the general direction we were heading toward, but that was the limited extent of our bushwhacking knowledge base of known values. We began to do the usual slow gait, picking our way along an imagined route, then turning back and retracing our steps, trying to "pick up the scent" once again, but the trail seemed to be nonexistent. More and more, the site markers were becoming less and less familiar. I was beginning to worry.

I asked Danny to let me see the map. I asked him more than once, but each time, he kept insisting that he knew the trail (such as it was) and he assured me that we were fine, just follow him (famous last words). I didn't like the sound of this, because it wasn't really all that clear he did know where he was going. He seemed just as lost as the rest of us, doubling back over and over again, and saying, "Oh, right, here it is," then, "Oh, no, this is it, I'm sure of it." Not very encouraging at all.

I began to get angry at Danny, and I insisted we pull out the map and check where we were as best we could against the topography and our last best guess of where we left the visible, known trail. I was getting disoriented, and I did not like this feeling. We seemed to be going in circles, and yet, none of the terrain looked familiar.

Finally, Danny relented and pulled out the map, but when he did, he did it his way, not the way an experienced, knowledgeable hiker should do it. Danny pulled out an old, tattered map that looked like it had been in the back pocket of his jeans for the last three years, through all the laundry washings.

I saw the condition of the map as he pulled it out of his pocket, and my heart alternately sank, then inched its way up into my throat. I found a large rock nearby and told him to bring his map and let's spread it out fully on the rock.

But he said no need to do that. He proceeded to fold up the map into the tiniest rectangle possible, actually much smaller than what he had had in his pocket, and placed it in the palm of his hand. He looked at the map in his palm, looked around a bit, pointed to a ridge off in the distance, then said: "Let's go this way." I said: "What?!"

We had no point of reference. He never tried to determine our location. He barely looked at the map, which itself was barely open to some undisclosed location in the High Sierra. I couldn't even be sure he had the right quadrant for this area. I knew nothing, and Danny knew next to nothing, as far as I could tell. I looked at the others and tried not to convey my fears nor my dismay. But I think they all knew something was very wrong here.

The situation only got worse. Danny continued taking us on dead-end routes, bushwhacking through dense undergrowth and thick forested areas. There was supposed to be a trail we should have been on, and the trail should not be taking us through this kind of closed vegetation, no matter if it was not maintained. It should have been a relatively open route. Not marked, okay, but still, we were not supposed to need machetes and chain saws to get through any part of this trail.

Every time I insisted we stop and study the map, *study the map, not glance at it*, Danny would pull it out of his pocket without bothering to open it, thrust it in the palm of his hand toward my face for about three seconds, then say to me: "Okay, you satisfied? We're right here [index finger jabbing some unknown point]. We're doing fine. I know this trail."

I began getting more angry as my panic level began to increase. The others began to panic as well. Fred's son started to cry. I imagined all manner of disaster headlines in the local newspapers. I imagined us out there all night, with dwindling sandwiches and granola bars, and a typical summer High Sierra storm drenching us or even covering us in a late but not unusual snowstorm. I wondered if this was how the people in the Donner Party felt, in those first hours when the full weight of their awful predicament began to choke all reason out of their heads.

At one point, Fred and his son decided they had had enough of Danny and his arrogant guiding (or lack of it). Fred announced that they were going to strike out on their own, in the direction that they believed we should be going. I wondered if I should join them, but Danny was the only one with a map, and the scenario most present in my consciousness involved knocking Danny out with a rock and taking that map and figuring out our way back to the trail.

Danny could find his own way when he regained consciousness, I figured. He seemed quite confident in himself, so worrying about him was not part of my plan. I just wanted to get my hands on that map.

I don't know how we managed to make it to the campsite, many hours late and just moments—literally moments—before dusk set in. It is a blur. The food and water had run out. We were famished, thirsty, and fatigued. I vaguely recall that Danny relented and handed me the map at some point, and somehow we found our way, or a reasonable substitute thereof. We heard a horse off in the distance and smelled a campfire starting up. Then, as we got closer to where our senses were leading us, we heard voices. We had arrived—exhausted, starving, dehydrated, and embittered by our experience, but safe.

Fred and his son were not there yet. I told Bill what we had endured, and we discussed sending out a search party before it got too dark. As we were making final preparations to find the missing father and son, we saw a head appear over the near ridgeline; it was Fred, and then we saw his son. They seemed to haul themselves toward us with the last ounce of strength left in them. We ran toward them with water and granola bars.

Fred told us he had considered finding a sheltered place under a rock to settle in for the night. But his son had started crying again, so he decided they should try a little while longer, at least while there was still some light. We must have all been guided in our most dire straits by the same fear to find the others. Bill began dishing out prepared meals and putting burgers on the grill. We wolfed them down like, well, like wolves. We turned in early that night, almost as soon as the last light faded. No one was up for campfire games at the moment.

But the next morning, dawn broke cold and clear, and Bill and I, always the two early birds in all of our camping adventures, made lots of rich dark coffee and hot cocoa, and that drew out the others from their slumbering bags and tents.

As the sun cleared the ridgeline and warmed up the site, our heads cleared and our attitudes improved, and everyone began the healing process of lingering in the details of our adventure yesterday, relishing the danger and downplaying the risk. We all began to put it in perspective and enjoy it from a safe distance now, and that was as it should be.

Before long, the boys were out at the edge of the river, casting their fishing lines. It did not take very long before they were catching fish, and we quickly gutted and filleted them and set them on the pan in some butter, alongside another pan of scrambling eggs. Then, we combined the fish and eggs, turning them in together, for one of the best meals I have ever had on a "rugged, roughing-it" camping trip. This was as it should be.

We spent three glorious days there, eating fish right out of the river until we got tired of it, wading in the stream when the sun got too hot, living a charmed life in the range of light, and grateful that our adventure was now one for the books and not for the newspaper headlines. Bill even managed, somehow, to pick up part of the Giants baseball game one afternoon, and we sipped our beer made cold in the high mountain stream while the boys ran around on the rocks like little lizards. When it was time to leave our mountain hideaway, we all followed the packtrain down.

This was what we came for, and all was forgiven with Danny. Well, almost all forgiven. I wouldn't do another trip with him again if my life depended on it. Because it did depend on him, and it almost ended badly. But on this trip, as in everything, although I may have been too worried and too tired to remember her name and keep my faith, my guardian angel was always here with us, in the High Sierra, as we stood a little bit closer to heaven at 11,000 feet.

I have not returned to those mountains in a long while. Bill is not able to do that kind of demanding adventure anymore. Danny is no longer with us, and the boys are all grown to men, making their own treks and adventures. But in my mind, late at night, I often wonder how it was that we were so lost for so long, and then, when things seemed at their bleakest, the smell of a campfire, the sound of voices, and the lingering dusk beckoning us to home in the High Sierra.

My Mother's Unshakeable Faith

It's easy to have faith in a benevolent God when your relationship to the Almighty all your life has been one of deliverance from harm, shelter in the storm, and, in very real and everyday events, redemption from your sins and limitations. This is how I would define my relationship with the divine and my faith.

It is much more challenging, I know, to maintain your faith in God and your perseverance in the face of adversity when your life has been repeatedly bludgeoned by trauma and plagued by troubles.

My mother has had a difficult life, or at least, this is what it seems like to me. She was three years old when her mother died, and her father was not fit to care for a large family all alone. He drank a lot; didn't have a job, like many people during the time of the Great Depression; and went missing from his kids for days and weeks at a time. For the rest of my mother's formative years, until she struck out on her own at the age of seventeen, her ten brothers and sisters were scattered to the four winds, separated and divided among the aunts and uncles. No one could take all of them under their wings.

My mom and her two younger twin brothers, Ray and Anthony, my namesakes, were sent off to live with an aunt, Delfina, who was not married, a spinster who, though kind enough to take in these three young children, was not really what one could reasonably call "mother material." The stories Mom has told us about those years with Aunt Delfina describe a life of "spare the rod and spoil the child," and the harsh conditions of living in the house of someone who never really wanted children.

Mom was always kind in her own way when she described those years, and—she was always quick to remind us—at least she had a roof over her head and food at the table every day. Because she does remember well how difficult her life was living on the streets before Delfina took them in. She and her kid brothers, the twins were, essentially, "street urchins," living at the mercy of the kindness of strangers, going hungry for days at a time, never knowing when their father would show up, or in what condition.

I know my mother had a rough start to her life, more difficult than I ever had, and I understand many of the root causes of her short temper, her impatience, her inability to mother me in the way I needed, and her over-reliance on corporal punishment to control our behavior.

I understand her now. I may seem harsh in my judgment of how she treated me, but I am merely being direct and clear in what I saw and felt at the time. These are my perceptions, after all, and I have a right to them. I own them. What I find more difficult to comprehend and fully appreciate is how well she managed to keep on forging ahead, her determination to press forward, the resiliency of her character, and her unshakeable faith that ultimately, things would get better, when it must have seemed that nothing could ever go right in her life.

In her love relationships, in her financial affairs, in her role as a mother and caregiver, she always seemed to me to be born under a bad sign. Yet, through it all, she always trusted that her life would, someday, be better, and that God was watching over her. She must have had as powerful and dutiful a guardian angel as I have, one that kept whispering loudly in her ear: *I will watch over you always.*

But what can explain her belief in the Roman Catholic Church, when the church betrayed her in a most insidious way at a time when she was most vulnerable? The Roman Catholic Church did my mom a very dishonorable deed, stealing from her, and I cannot forgive them for what they did to her.

When my mom was in her fifties, divorced from Raul by now and with a full-time job working at General Hospital in Los Angeles, she decided that she wanted to enter a convent and devote her life to God. She wanted to be a "bride of Christ," as the expression goes. I know it sounds crazy; we thought it was ridiculous. But my mom did her best to convince us that it was a sound, practical life choice, if you look at it from the financial side of things.

My mom reasoned that if she lived as a nun, the Church would care for her fully in her old age. Housing, medical care, food, clothing, and a retirement home when she was no longer able to get around on her own. She was also, in my view, fanatically religious, and she told us that she had always wanted to be a nun, although this was the first time any of us had ever heard her express this sentiment.

Mom faced an uphill struggle trying to explain to us her position on this bizarre decision, and we all became even more adamantly against it when we learned what she would have to do in order to gain entry to a convent.

If a convent accepted her, she would have to sign over to the church her entire life savings, including her pension funds. The Roman Catholic Church calls it the "dowry," from "brides of Christ," and the church's economic justification was that they were going to be footing the bill for all of her life expenses, and she had to give them what she had, since they would be spending a lot of money on her over time. They rationalized it as a necessary manifestation of the vow of poverty that men and women of the cloth must take, along with chastity and obedience. It is matter of common practice for many religious orders of the church. Mom had a nice little public employees' retirement pension working at General Hospital for the city and county of Los Angeles.

We thought it was a rash idea, and we didn't want her to go, but she brushed off our concerns and went ahead with her plans. Jo Ann, in particular, was upset that Mom would not be able to see her grandchildren growing up. Mom was unfazed; but then, Mom was not ever really the sweet little old grandma type, and she would be the first to admit it.

One day, Mom got word that a community of nuns at a convent in Indiana would accept her. She followed up with them and did whatever she had to do to get in, and that was that. She made her way to the convent, signed away all her money and financial security and put on the habit of a novitiate for her year of initiation. I still have a picture of Mom in her white and blue novice's habit. She doesn't look too happy, I must say.

Mom left the convent after six months. She had been treated badly, she told us, and she could no longer tolerate it. It was not the holy experience Mom was seeking. Mom was crushed. They kept her money too. When she asked them to return it to her, they told her they had spent it all.

Her sister, my Aunt Lucy, sent Mom a ticket home. She stayed with me for a while in the house in San Francisco I was sharing with Bill and Alan. I told her she could stay as long as she wanted. How ironic that now I was taking Mom in after the church had made her feel so unwelcome, after she had rejected me at birth and then kicked me out of the house when I was a kid. Life goes full circle in the strangest ways.

Mom was a mess. She cried all the time. She was a lost soul. She told me that the nuns were cruel to her, they were racist against Mexican

Americans. They made her scrub the toilets all the time. They used to sing "La Cucaracha" when she came walking down the hall. What sickness. I thought she was an idiot for going, but I couldn't help but feel sorry for her now. I understood the heartbreak of a broken dream.

It seemed to me a racket of the worst type imaginable—something only the Roman Catholic Church could dream up. To take a person's life savings, then boot them out, penniless and brokenhearted. She took a vow of poverty, all right, when she signed on at the convent, and they doomed her to a life of poverty ever since. After she left the convent, Mom was forced to start all over again, working and building up what meager savings she could pull together before old age took her out of the workforce.

I have never forgiven the church for their treatment of her. I looked into the possibility of any redress or return of the money, but it was futile. I spoke to a lawyer, and he told me the Roman Catholic Church has armies of the best lawyers in the world, and Mom had given them her money of her own free will, so she had no one to blame but herself. The Church had got one over on Mom, but it never dimmed her faith in "Holy Mother Church." But then, my mom's understanding of motherhood has always been a bit warped, in my view. The irony is not lost on me. I don't understand why the church would need to take my poor mom's money. While the income of the highest-ranking clergy is a closely held secret, cardinals earn about $5000 per month, plus housing, plus meals, plus perks like free unlimited international travel, while ostensibly doing the "holy work" of the Roman Catholic Church, a rather vague and undefined term.

Meanwhile, the poorest of the poor in Nigeria and the Congo live on $1.90 per day, or $730 per year. One Catholic cardinal's annual salary could support at least eighty of these families. So it seems to me the Church believes that one cardinal's comfort is worth the life of eighty African families. I wonder what Jesus would say?

After my recovery from COVID, I felt the need to celebrate my faith and worship God in congregation with others. I eventually decided to attend a local Lutheran church. I appreciate the fact that Martin Luther was the first priest to publicly denounce the corrupt church practice of buying your way into heaven with indulgences, and the vast wealth that was a corrupting force on the Roman Catholic Church. For this, he was excommunicated.

Not much has changed in the church in the five hundred years since Luther nailed his ninety-five theses on the door of the church in Wittenberg, nor in the eight hundred years since St. Francis of Assisi assailed the corrupt and wealthy princes of the church. I would bet that today the church is even more wealthy and no less corrupt.

I was pleased to find, in my Lutheran church, that the pastor never used the pulpit to admonish his parishioners to give more-more-more in the donation basket. They never pass the basket around. It stays in the back. He thanks the congregation once during the part of the service where he thanks God for all the blessings bestowed upon us, but he never tries to bully us to turn out our pockets for him. I found this to be a blessed relief from the constant harangues I remember at Sunday Mass in Resurrection Church when I was a child. In the barrio, no less, where the poorest of the poor reside.

I also respond well to the liturgy of hope, goodwill, and kindness that I hear from the Lutheran pulpit, and I remember well the gospel of fire and brimstone, punishment for our sins, purgatory and hell, and all the depressing rules of the Roman Catholic Church that kept us in fearful bondage of our wrathful God.

I attended a nondenominational church once with a friend long ago in San Francisco. Here, too, the sermon was basically all sweetness and light. The topic one Sunday was the Lord's Prayer, with a different interpretation of the words than I was taught in Resurrection School. The pastor told us that the ending of the prayer, which goes: "And deliver us from evil, amen," has been misinterpreted over time. She said it should read: "And deliver us from our limitations, amen."

Her reasoning was that there is no evil force incarnate in the world, personified in Satan or Lucifer, and God is not in a perpetual conflict against his archenemy till the end of time. The real struggle in this life that we each have within us is to overcome the limitations that hold us back from achieving the Godhead, from elevating ourselves beyond the shackles of the seven deadly sins so that we achieve the highest calling that is in our nature. Being the best that we can be. This is our path to enlightenment, not some epic duel with evil. Exceed our limitations.

We can't blame our failures on some outward force and say "the devil made me do it." We must work to go deep within ourselves to examine the root causes we own that hold us back from the goodness and happiness that is our right. The unexamined life is not worth living, as Socrates said before his execution. We should own our sins, not put it on the "devil"—the personification of evil. This makes so much more sense to me than the teachings I grew up with that only seem to hold us in abject bondage like children who constantly fear the rod.

My God is not a vengeful God. I put my faith in a benign, benevolent, and loving God, as manifest in the protective wings of my guardian angel that surround me at all times. My guardian angel said she would *watch over me* to keep me out of harm's way, far from the cliff. She does not *watch me* to make sure I stay on the straight and narrow.

It seemed to me the Roman Catholic Church could treat my mom in any way it liked, and she had an endless well of forgiveness. When Raul tried to kill her, and our pastor told her to "work things out." When she left the convent after six months, and they kept her life savings. When I pressed her on this, her response was always "that is not the church that I know and love." *But it is the church that is treating you badly, Mom.*

I wish Mom had had the same reservoir of patience and acceptance of my teenager's age-appropriate behavior when I was dating Carmen. If she had, she would not have thrown me out of the house as she did. But then, everything worked out fine for me, after all. So I guess I should just let that go. But it still can bother me to this day if I allow it to, I will admit. This is my struggle, I know.

I don't understand Mom, but it's a matter of her faith, and I do understand this. For example, I really do enjoy the great cathedrals of the world. I always make a point of attending a traditional Sunday Mass if I am in a city where there is a great cathedral. I have attended Sunday Mass in the great cathedrals of Mexico City; Toledo; Sevilla; Madrid; Santiago de Compostela; St. Peter's Basilica; Westminster Abbey; Santa Maria del Fiore in Florence; the abbey of Farfa, Italy; Chartres; and Notre Dame in Paris.

I was in Notre Dame for midnight Mass on Easter Sunday one year. I was standing at the back of the cathedral, up against the door because I had come in late and there was nowhere to sit. It was at the beginning of the ceremony, and the archbishop of Paris, wearing his gorgeous golden miter, was leading a huge entourage of bishops and deacons, subdeacons and altar boys, all dressed in their finest regal purple-and-gold brocade vestments made just for this occasion, walking slowly from the altar and up the center aisle to the back where I was standing.

The archbishop of Paris walked directly to me where I stood, his golden incense burner smoking, the choir just above me singing their hearts out. The archbishop looked directly into my eyes as he waved that gorgeous mammoth golden incense burner at me. I choked on the thick, fragrant frankincense, my tears welling up from the sweet smoke as I stared right back at the archbishop.

Perhaps I was supposed to lower my eyes and humble myself before the exalted pageantry, but I was too interested in mentally photographing each moment for my mind's eye. I was captivated by the absolute majesty of this glorious vision designed to inspire awe and wonder. I'm glad I did this. It's a moment I will never forget. And it was awesome and inspiring, the music truly uplifting. It works.

I can relate to the visual manifestation of these ornate rituals and monuments to God. I also enjoy listening to Gregorian chant when I attend Mass in a cathedral. The music was made for these stunning acoustic spaces that took centuries to build. I imagine the solitary monks composing those simple chords with quill pens on parchment in the scriptoria of the great abbeys during Europe's darkest ages.

The music and the churches are beautiful tributes to man's attempt to transcend our earthly state and pierce the veil of divinity through sight and sound, and who can argue with that? We are, after all, sentient beings.

At this writing, my mother is in her mid-nineties, and still going strong and healthy and sharp. It's quite an amazing feat for someone who had to struggle against the tide for all of her life. She lives alone and independent in a small apartment that is seniors only and low income, so she never pays more than a small, fixed percentage of her meager income. This is a good thing. We should all be so lucky. She has no real income after the convent took her retirement savings. So she landed on her feet, after all, and I am glad for that. She deserves some measure of peace and security after all that she has been through.

All of her ten brothers and sisters are gone now. She is the only one still alive. She talks about how things were when they were growing up, the same stories over and over again. I remember all of my aunts and uncles, now deceased, though I have not kept close to any of my cousins spread all over the western states, far from the place we all grew up, in Lincoln Heights and Boyle Heights, East Los Angeles. She was very close to her brothers and sisters, and I know she is not happy that I am not inclined to stay in touch with those cousins.

When I asked my mother once how she feels being the last surviving member of her family, she looked at me and said, in all sincerity and without a trace of sarcasm, "The good die young, the rest of us linger and have to suffer for our sins." Her answer came out in an instant, not a moment's hesitation, as if she had been preparing for this question all her life, her reply right there on the tip of her tongue, in case anyone ever asked.

I didn't know what to make of this comment, so I just shrugged and looked at her, trying to read her mind or her facial cues, but she sat there, a blank paper for me to write my own impressions of her words or, better still, a stone that reveals little more than its hard, cold surface.

I am left to believe that she imagines that she is the least of her family; not the best; that she has been left here to suffer even more than she had in the prime of her life—a life full of regrets, wasted efforts, dashed dreams, and lost family members. I don't know any more if it's a blessing or a curse that she still has her wits about her, that she still remembers so much with such clarity, and that she now has nothing but those memories and no one alive who cares about them as much as she did. She still tries to tell me how to live my life. This bothers me, still, so I spend as little time with her as I feel I can get away with, I have to admit.

Like the cruel joke that was my father's ultimate demise—slipping on a cherry tomato in the line at the casino salad bar—life has played a cruel joke of another nature on my mother: to keep her alive for a very long time with so much psychic pain and emotional loss still so clear in her mind.

Now, the walls of Mom's little furnished apartment are covered in old photos, photocopied images of old photos, yellow and ragged at the edges from too much handling—the little apartment that smells of urine and fried pork chops. I imagine Mom talks to those people on the walls, some people I hardly recognize anymore, people that mean so little to me now. The aunts and uncles who used to try to coax me to utter my first words back in the days when Mom thought I was stupid or developmentally challenged.

I wonder if she remembers the same things I remember. I wonder how she feels if she does recall. We have never, ever talked of such things. Why bother? I am satisfied with how my life turned out, and though I have not forgotten these wounds, I have, in my way, forgiven her. What good would it do to do otherwise? To hang on for a lifetime to such pain? I remember it now only as the stuff of my narrative, the stories I will tell to my grandchild about how not to be a parent.

I can imagine that my mom has conveniently, fortunately, forgotten such things. Or else she might be racked with guilt and regret for more than she already is. I wish that on no one. I am glad to retire to our neutral corners, out of the fray of old battles royale, away from the violence that was my childhood, for a life that now I prefer to keep full of peace and love and light. I tell myself that I love her in my way, the only way I know how.

It may be that, in my doting old age, I will be like my mother and retain a memory sharp as nails, quick as a fox, but ever careful to avoid the potholes and land mines that made up the war zone of my younger days, the days when I did not know any better, the days that are better left forgotten. I can only hope that someday, I will be reconciled to a life filled with contradictions. A life full of pain, while I still wear a smile on my face, and stare at the old photos on the wall, of people who were good and who died young.

I suspect this could be my destiny. I have the same body type as my mother. I have always followed the advice that she herself follows on matters of health and nutrition. She has always been right in this regard, and I have been the beneficiary of her good common sense. She used to delight in telling us when we were children that "we were bred of hardy mongrel stock." I never quite understood the implications of these words, but now they make perfect sense. And so, again, I do thank her for the good she imparted to me as a child, for her DNA, as I thank her for setting me free so young—at birth, even—so that I may pursue my own life, my own dreams, my destiny.

Sonny did tell me on the night before we buried him that I would live to be a very old and happy man. It seems that this has become my mother's destiny. I certainly hope so, for her sake, as well as for mine. We cannot pick the family that we are born to. We can only make the best of the cards we are dealt and, over time, find the family that we need.

I remember when we were kids and attended Mass with Mom every Sunday at Resurrection Church. When we arrived inside the church, dipping our fingers in the holy water font inside the entrance and making the sign of the cross with our wet fingers, Mom would cover her head with her black lace shawl and push us along the center aisle, telling us to go take a pew in the front, close to God.

Mom, however, always hung back, taking a seat in the very last pew of the church. She always did this. And, whenever I stole a look backward at her, she was always kneeling in solemn prayer, her head bowed low, gently shaking from side to side, engaged in a quiet soliloquy with God and the heavenly host.

Once, when I was older, well into my thirties and comfortable about talking with my mother in an adult way on matters of the church and faith,

I asked her why she never came up to the front of the congregation with us when we were younger, like all the other parents would do, the whole family sitting together, celebrating their faith side by side.

She opened up to this question. By then she and I had figured out a way to have serious conversations about important things, always careful not to venture too close to the painful subjects, always talking around the most pressing concerns that haunted us both about our relationship and what each of us had suffered through together. "I always sat in the back because I am not worthy of God's love," she told me. "I am a sinner, and I don't deserve to put myself close to the tabernacle. I am like the centurion in the Bible who said to Jesus Christ: *'Lord, I am not worthy to have you come under my roof; but only speak the word, and my servant will be healed'" (Matt 8:8).*

This hurts me in ways too profound to describe. It gives me a fuller sense of the pain my mother has experienced throughout her life, and makes her one of the most human and vulnerable people I have ever known. For my mother, her whole life seems to have been about *mea culpa, mea culpa, mea maxima culpa*—"through my fault, through my fault, through my most grievous fault." I am sorry she carries such a burden of guilt and shame for the sins she feels she has committed.

There it is again. My mother suffers the same affliction, the same addiction my father did. The sickness of self-loathing, which renders her incapable of forgiving herself and moving on, and condemns her to a life of never feeling good enough to stand proud in her own skin. Where my father sought to escape from himself in a different reality in drugs, booze, women, and gambling, my mother sought her refuge in a state of perpetual penitence, in always ripping the scab off the old wounds.

I don't know why my mother could not accept the doctrine of confession as fully as she embraced her original sin. But then, sin is cleansed from our souls in confession, while we are still doomed to pay the price, to atone for our sins, to pay the debt once we acknowledge our sins, by burning in purgatory. This is a closed loop of misery. To forgive but not to forget.

For Mom, the teachings of the Church are all about our journey in this vale of tears, the *vallis lacrimarum* of early Christian doctrine. Original sin has cursed us from birth to a life of constant "do-over," of being marked at the moment we are born with the sign of the devil through no fault of our own, Adam and Eve's one and only transgression that caused God to cast them from the garden of Eden. This reminds me of my only sin of dating

Carmen, which resulted in Mom throwing me out of the house. No second chance. One mistake, and you're out of here.

In my mom's worldview, we spend the rest of our lives repenting and apologizing for a transgression for which we are not responsible, the sins of the father and mother. In this paradigm, there is no such thing as an innocent newborn. We come into this world already a sinner, always being forced to play "catch-up" in God's eyes. Guilty, even at birth.

It is an awful cross to place on the tiny shoulders of those who least deserve it. My mother grew up in this belief system, a system that made sure we are always aware of our unworthiness to enjoy God's love, always aware of our sinful natures, our unworthiness to be happy in the knowledge of joyful innocence.

In the Roman Catholic Church, the litany of "mortal" and "venial" sins we are prone to is immense. It seems impossible to ever be comfortable in our humanness, in our weakness, to cut ourselves any slack. For if we were to die in a state of mortal sin, we would go straight to hell and suffer for eternity in the fire and brimstone that awaits us there, never to delight in the heavenly bliss and peace of God's good grace.

It is a cruel system that seems designed to hold us in bondage, the lifelong tally of our transgressions in the eyes of God, like Jacob Marley in *A Christmas Carol*, wearing a long trail of chains that he was condemned to drag behind him for all eternity, the overwhelming and inhumane burden we carry forever.

My mother felt that she was far beyond redemption for the sins she committed in her youth. Perhaps she felt that the proof of her unworthiness was the continued suffering she had to endure: the early death of her eldest son; the emotional loss of her second son; the death of Ernie, her only true love; her horrible, unloving marriage to Raul; and all the other travails and losses she has witnessed in her long life.

> *Stabat Mater dolorosa iuxta crucem lacrimosa dum pendebat filius.*
> The grieving mother stood weeping beside the cross where her son was hanging.
> —Jacopone da Todi, thirteenth century

I know well the teachings of the Roman Catholic Church, and I have seen firsthand how these doctrines were always more about the stick than the carrot, more threat than enticement, more mean than joyful. My mother was always trapped in original sin, always atoning for the undeserved mark of the devil.

I feel bad for her and how, in her old age, she has never grown beyond the paradigm of that young woman sitting in the very last row of Resurrection Church, unworthy to be sitting with the rest of the congregation, wearing the scarlet letter for all to see, a sinner among the anointed, cast out from the heavenly host.

I can only hope that, someday, when Mom is on her deathbed, she receives the last rites while she is still alert, aware, and cognizant that all her sins, from birth to death, have finally been fully and completely washed away with the holy water and oil, so that she may know, at long last, that she is worthy to enter the kingdom of heaven and leave this vale of tears.

My prayer is that, one day, long before she is on her deathbed, she does come to learn what it means to be free, as she showed me long ago how to be free—free of guilt, free of regret, free of bitterness. I keep the faith, for my mother's sake, that freedom, peace, and redemption will be her ultimate fate.

Perhaps I sensed, in seeing the misery of my parents' lives, their self-loathing, that a strong sense of self, a good healthy ego, and a faith in my own wits was the key to my salvation. After all, life itself is a matter of faith, and of keeping faith in the face of all adversity, tragedy, and pain. Indeed, ironically, faith of a certain kind has been my mom's strength all her life. I can see that with all that she has had to deal with, she, too, has been protected and watched over. I have come to realize that, yes, my mom has always had her own guardian angel, standing close by, whispering in her ear: *I will watch over you always, as I have watched over your son since you gave him over to my care on the day he came into this world.*

The Day I Spent with Muhammad Ali

Happy birthday to the King! Today is January 17, and it is Muhammad Ali's birthday, and I will never forget the day I spent with him.

It was 1986, and I was working in public relations at Children's Hospital Oakland. One day we got a call that Ali wanted to come visit the kids. I was assigned the task of setting up the meetings with the various departments and escorting Ali and his small retinue throughout the hospital.

Ali had been diagnosed recently with Parkinson's disease, but already the symptoms were manifest. He could barely talk and his hands shook, but his smile was huge and his energy was strong and his will was overwhelming.

All the adults in the hospital who met Ali on that day were thrilled to see him, but the kids really had no idea who he was. They did respond to the love and joy in his face as he took time with each one of them. Most of the kids were terminal, diseases of all kinds, the toughest cases in all of Northern California.

This was not a publicity stunt. We were asked not to promote it to the media. Ali was not seeking attention from the public. He wanted only to spend the day with the kids.

Muhammad Ali was with us that whole day. It's a day I will always cherish. Ali was a hero to me and not only because he was the greatest heavyweight boxer of all time, but because he spoke truth to power, fought the draft to Vietnam, even when it cost him everything he worked for his entire life—the heavyweight title, all the money he spent on lawyers' fees and court costs. The hatred of angry racist people who found another excuse to talk trash about him.

Like so many other young men at that time, I did not want to fight in this unjust war. Ali helped us articulate our objections. He was a powerful symbol of black resistance, one of the few professional athletes to use his public platform to oppose the war and to sacrifice everything to do so, like John Carlos and Tommie Smith at the 1968 Olympics.

Happy birthday, Ali. You are the greatest. May you always float like a butterfly and sting like a bee. You and this precious memory we shared will be with me always.

Long COVID

It has been almost two years since I got deathly ill with the plague in January 2021. I could tell you to the day and the hour how long it has been since my death watch. I keep a close watch on time now and how it moves with the seasons, with the sun and the moon, with the body count worldwide, with the tides in my blood, and with my breath, in and out, in and out, just to make sure I am still alive.

But you don't really need to know such particulars. Most peoples' eyes glaze over when I bring up such granular specifics, such minute details. The days, the hours, the minutes that have passed from then until now. They are of little interest to most people. But to me, they mean the world.

At this writing, more than two years since the beginning of this plague, more than six and a half million people in the world have died—more than one million in the U.S. One million Americans dead in just twenty-four months. It takes twenty-five years to lose one million lives on America's highways.

For this is my world now. This is the world of post-plague, the afterworld of this disease, the effects of long COVID, and what may be waiting for me just around the corner, lurking in the shadows beyond that next bend in the road. For we have learned that once you're over COVID, you're still not over it. It is a most peculiar disease, with a half-life like plutonium. It seems it never goes away.

I read everything I can about the known problems the research is turning up about the long-term effects of this plague on the body. It's my body, and it concerns me. I had it bad, and I wonder, almost every day and hour, how bad it might be, if it isn't over yet.

And this is what I keep learning, in my almost obsessive preoccupation with the possibilities that, although I may have escaped death in the hospital, I may not be out of the woods yet. Despite the fact that I arose from my deathbed miraculous like Lazarus from the tomb, there is still a good possibility that the plague may get me still.

Here is the thing I find most strange about COVID. The disease itself, when your body is locked in the throes of it, presents in the body as well-known respiratory ailments, such as viral pneumonia or pulmonary emboli, which are blood clots in the lungs. Modern medicine knows how to treat these conditions; we have the medicines and the established protocols.

But once the disease has run its course in the body, and the patient is treated, cured, and recovering, there is the risk of long COVID, and these ailments are less understood, or rather, no one really knows which conditions will occur in the body, or in what combination, or when, or for how long. It's like cancer that doesn't go away.

They keep learning something new, some new danger that is uncovered for even those who had a mild case. These conditions are found more often in people who had a severe case of the plague. They keep finding new problems that present in the body in the months after the patient is discharged: heart arrhythmia, heart palpitations, chronic fatigue, sleep problems, systemic organ failure, loss of feeling in the legs and arms, stomach pain, joint or muscle pain, chronic diarrhea, fever, and more. For some, the conditions may last for years. For years. And for years, these problems may lie dormant, a ticking time bomb. Time. I keep a close watch on time now.

As this plague drags on in the world, no doubt they will find more debilitating symptoms of long COVID as the number of the infected grows, as the body of research increases over time. For now, it seems frightening enough to me the things they know already. A ticking time bomb. Time. I keep time.

I must say I have been fortunate, so far. Other than an occasional cough that is easily remedied with a throat lozenge, I feel my recovery continues on a steady state, ever more progressive, onward, ever onward, back to full health and good conditioning. I keep a regular daily exercise program, and I am ever mindful of a healthy diet, as I did before I got sick. The condition of my body was a key factor in my recovery, my doctor told me, so I take that as a testament to the power of fitness and nutrition. This I have always believed in, and this was my affirmation.

So I would like to believe that my conditioning can ward off the most harmful effects of long COVID, can keep me safe from further harm. This is my prayer. This is my mantra. So far, it has proven useful. I feel, every day, stronger, more rejuvenated, more energized, more healthy. This is what a good fitness program should do for the body, and it is working. So far.

Still, I wonder, when I read the research, searching for some clue to my own unique, individual experience. I wonder if it will sneak through my defenses once again, as the plague once did when it first struck me down. I was careful then. I believed in the science. I did what I was told. I stayed as safe as I could. But I failed somewhere, somehow.

They talk a lot, in the medical journals, about problems with sleep that have affected people long after they got infected with the plague. I have my own unique, individual experience with a sleep condition that has come about since I got infected. And it is most bizarre.

Before I got sick, for much of my life, really, I had problems falling asleep at night. I would turn off the light, lay my head on the pillow, and lie there, thinking, trying not to think, trying to stop the continual dialogue, the constant din banging in my head, the problems of the day, the arguments I had, the noise in the moment on the street outside, the things I had to do tomorrow, the bills I had to pay, the work I had to do. The usual stuff.

This nonstop, relentless cacophony was my usual nighttime ritual, the clock ticking away the minutes, an hour, sometimes two. Until finally, fatigue set in, and I passed out, exhausted from the mental exertion. It always took me a long time to get to sleep at night. I got used to it.

Now, here is the odd thing about the plague, and I noticed it almost immediately after I was discharged from the hospital and home, safe in my own bed. Now—and there hasn't been one night this has not happened in all the time since I was discharged—now, I fall asleep almost immediately after I hit the pillow. If I were counting sheep, I would not get past number five, it is that sudden. Every night, I fall asleep immediately upon turning off the light and closing my eyes. I don't have a sleep problem, anymore. I have a staying-awake problem.

I have read as much as I can to see if this is a "thing." I feel I have read every published article with the word COVID in it. I have scoured the medical journals and googled "sleep conditions post-COVID." Nothing. It's all about normal healthy sleep patterns being disrupted by the plague. The sleep disorders they have encountered in patients who were infected are all about insomnia or waking up in the middle of the night. I have found nothing about falling asleep quickly and having a full night sleep on a regular basis.

I have developed my own theory about this change in my sleep patterns. I have wondered if my body is pleased to be home, safe, in my own bed, with all that danger behind me. I have considered the possibility that my muscle memory, my brain, remembers all those awful nights in the hospital when I never slept, literally never slept, with round-the-clock meds and injections, with machines constantly beeping and red and green lights flashing, and the chronic state of anxiety I was in that told me that if I allowed myself to fall asleep, I might never wake up. And now, now that those nights are gone, my body can, at long last, get a good, uninterrupted night's sleep.

I don't have an answer. It doesn't seem that anyone does. But if this is an effect of long COVID, then it is the strangest, most anomalous, most unique condition that I can find in the medical record. But who's to say what is normal, with a disease that is so new, so terrifying, and mutates constantly in so many ways? It seems like every case is different; the plague hits different people in different ways. It is a mystery, and only time will tell what lies ahead.

Time, I keep a close watch on time now, and how it moves with the seasons, with the sun and the moon, with the body count worldwide, with the tides in my blood and my breath, in and out. With every day I mark the calendar, and I check my vital signs, and I feel my body here and there for any telltale signs of distress. I go out on my bike or on my run, and I listen, and I watch for any warnings. Will this be the day, will this be the hour, will this be that moment, when my luck runs out?

And as I listen to the rhythm of my breath, as I run for any telltale signs of trouble, and when I hear the throbbing of my heart beating in my chest, the only sound I hear is the voice of my guardian angel, whispering in my ear, running there beside me, keeping close to me, her hand on my beating heart, saying to me quietly: *I will watch over you always*, words I have taken to heart, words I have always believed, words that never seem to fail me. And this is enough to put me at ease.

My Beautiful Big Blue House

Surely goodness and mercy shall follow me all the days of my life, and I shall dwell in the house of the Lord my whole life long.

—Ps 23

Fast-forward to the now, to time in the ever present, to current reality and a full lifetime both behind me and yet still ahead.

I BOUGHT A HOUSE IN Eureka recently. It's a very nice house, in excellent condition, with wonderful "curb appeal" and very well situated.

I am happy to be here and amazed that I have made this move. This was never in my plan. But it doesn't take a genius to see that it will be a good investment for me in the long term. In the short term, however, buying another house was never what I had in mind.

It was quickly evident to me, beyond any doubt, from the moment the opportunity appeared for me to buy this house, that, once again, the hand of our Creator was all over this plan. It is yet another example of my guardian angel wrapping her protective wings around me and my sister Jo Ann, the little boy and girl in that image on my mother's bedroom wall a lifetime ago, in a place and a world far away.

I never wanted to own a house again at this late stage in my life. Why bother with the concerns and the woes of homeownership? Buying a home requires a major up-front capital investment, down payment, fixing up problems before move-in, with the payback coming over a long period of time.

And then there are the often and inevitable expenses of maintenance. I know. I owned a home in San Francisco for twenty-five years. I took good care of that house, it was a good house, but it did cost money every year for simple routine maintenance. Money that a renter never has to pay. Money I would have preferred to keep in my pocket for my travels once again when the plague has lifted off our world. I had other plans for my money in my golden years.

I reasoned that equity in a home takes twenty to twenty-five years to build. The initial mortgage payments of a new homebuyer are more than 98 percent interest. The payback in equity is far down the road, further than I could ever hope to realize at my age.

My dream at this point in my life was to live as a renter in this town where the cost of renting is very affordable. Keep my cash close at hand. Save my money in hand for the things I want to enjoy while I can. My granddaughter's college expenses. A new and comfortable car. World travel. Good food, good wine, the good life. Sinking lots of my available cash into a down payment on a house really makes no financial sense at this late stage of my life. It still doesn't, even though I went ahead and bought. Home ownership is not for everyone.

But plans are what we do. And life is what happens.

I was renting a nice little apartment at the back of the property of a wonderful couple, Diane and Cathy, who live in the front of the property. Both older, like me. Both dear friends, long-time "family" to my sister, Jo Ann, who has lived next door for more than forty years. I had been living in this nice little apartment since moving to Eureka three years ago after I returned to the States from my Italian expat adventure.

So far, so good. I was paying a very easy rent, with no obligation to maintain the property. I was free to travel wherever and whenever I wanted. And I did. There was my three-month return visit to Italy just before the plague struck. I also stayed in San Francisco for three months—just before the plague struck me down—to take care of Bill when he was not well.

I had planned to return to this free and easy life after the plague. And aside from almost dying from COVID, things were humming along quite nicely.

Then life happened, once again. Diane passed away. She had been in a bad way for a while, and she finally gave it up. A year later, Cathy, her partner of forty years, followed her out of this life. It's eerie how long-term partners will do that; one dies, and the other one soon follows. I have seen this happen more times than I can deny it as mere coincidence. Cathy and Diane had no heirs, and in their will they dictated that everything be sold and the proceeds allocated to some charities of their choosing.

At this point, I realized that my sweet little rental deal might soon disappear. Tenants have no rights in this county. I had to either find another place to rent and pay almost four times what I had been paying, or make an offer to buy this property and permanently live next door to my sister.

It was a no-brainer. I prayed on this for a few days, then made an offer that the trust administrator could not refuse; and the rest, as they say, is history. We closed escrow, and the deal was done.

For me, there is an even stranger aside to this story. This big beautiful blue house has a peaked roof—two of them, in fact—the main peaked roof plus a smaller peaked roof over the entrance steps leading up to the porch. This is the only house I have ever lived in that has a peaked roof. Big deal, you say.

Well, it is a big deal to me. When I was a child living in the barrio, every year on my birthday, my wish before I blew out the candles was to live in a house with a peaked roof. This went on for years. Everyone who was gathered around my birthday cake knew that I was making this same wish year after year, because as I sat there, the burning candles before me, I would close my eyes and make my wish while forming a little peaked roof with my two hands. I would whisper to myself: "This year, I wish we could live in a house with a roof like this" (hands forming a peak together). I didn't know the words *peaked roof*. I just made that little shape of the peak. It became a family joke, year after year.

Why did that little boy from the projects wish every year to live in a house with a peaked roof? Because the projects were built with flat roofs, ugly, blocky, cinder block public housing units. Somehow, that little boy managed to equate a home with a peaked roof as a metaphor for middle-class, comfortable living.

Little Ray saw on television that the happy families on TV lived in homes with peaked roofs—programs like *My Three Sons*, *Father Knows Best*, *Dennis the Menace*. These families dressed up for dinner, smiled at each other all the time. Big brothers hung out with their little brothers. No one tried to strangle anyone else to death.

I somehow understood deep within my consciousness that I lived in substandard public housing, a flat roof, and I wanted out of there and wished for the house with the peaked roof. That peaked roof represented to me a stable, loving, happy home life. I sensed my state of poverty, the misery I had experienced in those projects and beyond, and the peaked roof became my dream house. The home where peace and love would live. The peaked roof became a metaphor for the home and the home life that I wanted.

Now, at long last, for the first time in my life, I have a house with a peaked roof, a lifetime after I wished for one. Now, my sister and I will be living next door for the rest of our lives, supporting each other, caring for each other, having each other's back. She has been so alone since her daughter and husband were painfully ripped from her life. I know she draws some measure of comfort having me so close. I feel the same.

I shake my head when I look back at how rapidly the world shifted beneath our feet toward pain and trauma. Death is on my mind these days. The death in recent times of so many loved ones—of family and friends, of so many dreams, the dreams of so many lives. I am beginning to dream of death and all its raging faces.

I fear not my own fate, which I know will come eventually, inevitably. I fear not that someday I, too, will be but a dream; a memory; a flickering moment in the vast expanse of time; a brief name carved on a dusty, forgotten tombstone sitting on a hill overlooking the great blue sea.

What I fear more than my insignificant nothingness in years to come—that fate awaits us all—what I fear more than the great unknown is not that my life today will amount to nothing in some distant time and mean nothing in the great flowing river of our lives. I sit here in this moment dreading not my own end of life someday but that my life right now may have no meaning in this moment.

Not so strange to feel so insignificant in the long years after I am gone. This I am prepared to accept. What I refuse to admit is that I may have no relevance to the world in which I live as I live it now, day by day.

Today is what matters most, I feel. Today is what matters; tomorrow, come what may. I must make this moment count. Because ultimately, nothing else will mean a damn thing, will mean so much less than the cool wind swirling around my forgotten tombstone sitting on a hill overlooking the great blue sea.

I am grateful that some sense of balance and equilibrium has been restored in some ways when I closed escrow on this house. It will not make up, of course, for the losses we have endured and the "unbearable grief" Jo Ann will always suffer, but still, it seems that the world has righted itself in the best way possible.

In this home, alone at night, I gaze up at the ceiling in my bedroom, and I hear the words softly echo in the light breeze that blows the fog around outside my house—*I will watch over you always*—words that, once again, never seem to fail me. Words that I now can say to my little sister, as I live in this beautiful big blue house. My first house with a peaked roof. That little boy's wish has come true.

Flashback to a state of being, to a place in the distant past, a time before all that became, the time when I was an innocent. I think back to that little boy in the projects, living in a place where he could hear the sound of the church bells ringing on Sunday morning, the church of the resurrection.

I think back to that man in the hospital, the oxygen mask strapped to his face twenty-four-seven, hovering at the threshold of death. I remember the doctor telling me, days after I was discharged, that there were three occasions in the intensive care unit when he thought I would not survive the night. I cannot help but remember that, after three days in the sepulcher, Christ rose from the dead, according to the Scripture.

I say a silent prayer of thanks, for all that was and all that became for that little boy in the projects, sitting on the curb in the smog, staring at the hot asphalt, and hearing the sound of the church bells tolling every Sunday morning, at the church of the resurrection.

I am the resurrection and the life. Those who believe in me, even though they die, will live. (John 11:25)

In the House Made of Dawn

In the house made of dawn
In the story made of morning light
On the trail of dawn
Oh, male divinity,
My feet, restore for me,
My limbs, restore for me,
My body, restore for me,
My voice, restore for me.

Today, take out your spell for me,
Away from me, you have taken it.
Happily, I recover.
Happily, my insides become cool.
Happily, my limbs regain their power.
Happily, my head becomes cool.
Happily, I walk.

Impervious to pain, I walk.
Feeling light within, I walk.
With lively feelings, I walk.
With beautiful pollen in his voice
With beautiful pollen in my voice.

It is finished in beauty
It is finished in beauty
In the house of evening light
From the story made of evening light
On the trail of evening light.

—*Traditional Dineh Night Chant*

Epilogue

This is a memoir, which is defined as an historical account composed from personal experience or knowledge. I have made every effort to keep the facts as close to the truth as I can remember. Nothing has been embellished. Nothing has been glossed over. Every word in this memoir is true, as I remember it, rooted as it is in my own life experiences.

There are a few things we can say about memory. Memory is intensely personal, highly subjective, and also deeply flawed. Five people may have witnessed the same event, and years, or months, or even weeks later remember it differently, based on their own subjective experiences and interpretations. But there is another overriding and more potent fact in effect here, and that is the internal truth that comes from a person's deepest knowledge of his own nature, his own sense of values, and his own understanding of his place in the cosmos.

And while an autobiography is the story of a person's life, a memoir is a story of particular events or a particular time, of important turning points or touchstone moments in a life that have influenced the writer. This memoir I have written is a collection of vignettes—stories that are focused on vivid imagery and meaning, rather than on plot. The meaning I wish to convey, of course, is the benevolent hand of God throughout my life, as manifest in the enfolding, guiding, and protecting arms of my guardian angel every day, watching over me always.

I have hewn as close to the facts, as I recall them, as any man can, mostly to be honest about what I have seen and lived, but also to be as clear as humanly possible about the lessons that I have learned as a result of the experiences in my life. There may be others in my family or in my life who may not recall these facts exactly as I have presented them. I have no doubts about this, and it is to be expected, especially in families.

My sister Jo Ann, for example, will certainly take issue with some of the memories as I recall them, especially in matters concerning my mother. In fact, we have already disagreed on certain "facts," as we each recall them, when I have checked in with her from time to time as I was writing this memoir. This is to be expected, not only because siblings can have very different recollections of the events they experienced together as children but also because my sister and I have very different attitudes and very different relationships to Mom.

Jo Ann and Mom have always gotten along together very well. They are very similar in many ways, I have come to see through the years, although my sister, no doubt, would feel differently. This is to be expected. And one reason they get along so well, in my opinion, is that Mom has always tended to treat Jo Ann in a very special way, other than the way Mom has treated me. The reason for this is simple, and I have come to accept it without remorse or rancor. It just is what it is.

Jo Ann is Ernie's daughter—the child of the one and only man whom Mom ever truly loved. Jo Ann has always been special in our family, not only as the youngest child for almost a decade, and not only as the only daughter for the same length of time but mostly because she is Ernie's daughter, the love child. I mean this in all kindness. I, on the other hand, was the "accident," the child Mom and Dad never wanted, the child Mom decided to give up before I was born, the child Mom thought was defective, mute, stupid. The child Mom must have regretted taking back from the foundling hospital when she realized I was such damaged goods. Jo Ann, on the other hand, was always and ever the love child.

So when Jo Ann and I have those conversations where we compare notes about our childhood as it relates to Mom's behavior or how she treated us, it comes as no surprise to me that we have vastly different recollections of what we think happened, each memory tainted by the subjective experience of who we were in our mother's eyes, of how we were loved or not loved, of how we were treated or mistreated. This is to be expected. It is what it is.

I have written the words on these pages because they have been inscribed within my heart and soul since the earliest years of my life, and only recently have I found the will and the compelling urge to share them with others. Just as I have learned to live my own life, accepting that no one else "gets me," I can only hope that others can accept my reality for what it is. My life. My truth.

I say this out of a profound sense of humility and appreciation for the good in my life—and the "bad"—that has come my way. I am glad to have lived this life God has given me; I have been blessed far more than any man can hope for, but I will take it all as graciously as I can, the good and the not-so-good, and I hope in my final days on earth I will still have a smile on my face and a positive, accepting, and gracious attitude for whatever is yet to come my way.

This ride isn't over yet. I feel there remains plenty more to come, *inshallah*. I have merely decided to take this moment, at long last, to capture it in the written word, because I am, after all, a writer. This is who I am and who I have been since that little boy of five uttered those first words of defiance to his mother, asserting who he is: not a deaf-mute as she suspected but, on the contrary, a person who observes and waits for the moment that is his, the moment in which he is ready to tell his story. I am a writer, and a writer, as we all know, has to write—sincerely, audaciously, and bluntly—the truth that he perceives in his experience.

Finally, it must be said, if anything is to be learned from a lifetime of experience, of salvation, of redemption, that I bear no ill will toward anyone in my life whom I may have represented in these pages as "doing me wrong." Parents, lovers, employers—fate, betrayals, mistreatments, wrongs, hurts. For although I have described certain events as painful, or destructive, or harmful to me in some way at the time, today, ultimately, everything in my life—everything—has turned out to be all for the better. This memoir is not a list of grievances but a testament to the power of faith—in God and in myself. I see every experience has been a good lesson for me, ever the student. I am here, I am happy, I am sane, and I am whole, and living to write about it with joy in my heart.

The things I have said here are not meant to blame others for supposed wrongdoings but merely to point out that the setbacks I have experienced have somehow turned into advantages for me, thanks to my guardian angel, to a higher power, to the strength that I derived from each blow I received, to get up again and move on with my life, adapting to change as I went along. So I carry no grudges, no bitter remorse, no resentment even to those who "did me wrong." Because, in the end, in beauty it is finished.

I got my college degree in English, because as a child I had always been a voracious reader. My appetite for literature only grew as a result of my university education. I learned much about life and how to cope with it in the written words of others. James Baldwin once wrote: "You think your pain and your heartbreak are unprecedented in the history of the world, but then you read." For much of my life I felt that no one has suffered as I have. But I read. Then I understood. And now I write, so that others may understand.

Despite the many issues between us, I have forgiven my mom because I know she tried her best with the cards she was dealt at the time. I thank my mother for setting me free on the day I was born. My life has been far richer, I am sure, for the independence she gave me at birth. I forgive, as well, everyone else whom I have represented as having done me wrong. I hope everyone whom I have wronged in my life forgives me for my transgressions. I did the best I could in the moment, and I am sorry I could not do better at the time. This is the best I can offer now. "I believe in the forgiveness of sins, the resurrection of the body, and the life everlasting."

I thank my guardian angel for coming off that wall on my mother's bedroom and for being real and present and always watching over me. I could not have done it without her help. She said these words to that little boy in the projects in a place long ago, in a time far away: *I will watch over you always*—words that I have always taken to heart, words that I have always believed, words that have never seemed to fail me. In beauty it is finished.

Bibliography

Baldwin, James. "The Doom and Glory of Knowing Who You Are." *Life* 54 (May 24, 1963).
Bourdain, Anthony. *Medium Raw*. New York: Ecco, 2010.
Paz, Octavio. *The Labyrinth of Solitude*. New York: Grove, 1961.
Rundell, Katherine. "What John Donne Knew about Death Can Teach Us a Lot about Life." *New York Times*, Sept. 10, 2022. https://www.nytimes.com/2022/09/10/opinion/john-donne-death.html.

www.ingramcontent.com/pod-product-compliance
Lightning Source LLC
Chambersburg PA
CBHW072136160426
43197CB00012B/2135